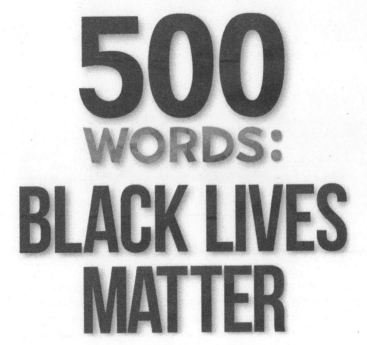

500 WORDS:
BLACK LIVES MATTER

A STUDIO PRESS BOOK

First published in the UK in 2020 by Studio Press,
an imprint of Bonnier Books UK,
The Plaza, 535 King's Road, London SW10 0SZ
Owned by Bonnier Books,
Sveavägen 56, Stockholm, Sweden

www.studiopressbooks.co.uk
www.bonnierbooks.co.uk

3 5 7 9 10 8 6 4 2

Cover illustration and internal design elements © Kyle Rowe
Edited by Laura Pollard, Sophia Akhtar, Frankie Jones and Helen Wicks
Designed by Rob Ward

Printed and bound in the UK.

CHRIS EVANS

ANGELLICA BELL   MICHAEL UNDERWOOD

500

WORDS:

BLACK LIVES
MATTER

5oo Words

Black lives Matter

CONTENTS

INTRODUCTION

" Dear Reader,

This book is a collection of some of the best entries that we had in this edition of the competition. Reading back through these stories, we are blown away by the passion, creativity and poignancy of the writing. The topic of Black Lives Matter was chosen to enable conversations, learning and provide an outlet for children to use their voices creatively to explore these crucial global issues, and this is something we have definitely seen.

We are excited to be working alongside the children's literacy support charity Coram Beanstalk, with all the profits from the sale of this book being donated to them in order to further their mission – building readers for life.

500 Words: Black Lives Matter was an absolute whirlwind from start to finish and we cannot thank the writers, the judges, and everyone in between enough!

The work does not stop here, so make sure you keep writing and using your voice for change.

See you next year! "

The 500 Words Team

CHRIS EVANS

" Three words: Black Lives Matter.

500 Words: The biggest children's writing competition on the planet. We know (because some very clever people at the Oxford University Press have told us) that 500 Words is the best indicator of what British kids are thinking about year on year. Trump led the charge back in 2017, then it was plastic and the environment, with Covid featuring this year even though it only came to light in the final couple of weeks of the main competition back in February. Our 500 Words: Black Lives Matter special however, has been a game changer.

First of all, it was conceived, executed and won all within the space of four weeks. Secondly, it is the first 500 Words where we have requested the nation's 5-3 year olds to write around a given theme.

As always, they didn't disappoint. What follows is an amazing and profound collection of some of our favourites.

Be prepared to laugh, sigh and cry.

Good luck and you might want to keep a tissue or two handy.

Thank you for supporting this and future 500 Words events by buying this book. "

MICHAEL UNDERWOOD

" When Chris first asked me to be involved in this spin-off of the 500 Words competition, I didn't know just how much it would be embraced by young people across the UK. What I did know, was I wanted to give those people a voice and an opportunity to share their thoughts and feelings about "Black Lives Matter" and the wider issue of systemic racism. The result is this incredible collection of stories, poems, and essays. They are honest, thought-provoking, and emotional. Chairing the judging panel was a real honour, as I got to see for myself the incredible variety and high quality of writing we received which made the judge's decision so difficult. Racism isn't going to stop overnight, but by everyone talking about it openly, and recognising there is a problem, we can move in the right direction. I'd like to thank all the schools who supported this competition and of course all the young people who took part, sharing their personal understanding about this important issue. "

ANGELLICA BELL

ᴸᴸ 2020 will always be a year I remember for many reasons and I think others will feel the same. One thing that struck me was how much I missed and loved people, my friends and even having general contact with strangers, so when it was highlighted that there still is so much division in the world brought to the forefront of the news by the death of George Floyd, it hit me hard. Being part of 500 Words – Black Lives Matter was incredibly important to allow our younger generation an outlet for them to vocalise their thoughts and stories on this global issue of racism using the power of words. We can look to the phrase "out of the mouths of babes" to understand often it's our young people that bring wisdom and clarity in difficult situations, and they didn't disappoint. Thank you to all those who engaged with the project. Thank you to all those who messaged me about it. And thank you to those who love unconditionally. We will get there. **ᵖᵖ**

PRAISE FOR 500 WORDS: BLACK LIVES MATTER

" The empathy and observation within these stories is truly inspiring. These children's understanding of the world around us and the changes that need to be made, give me real hope for the generation of tomorrow. **"**

   – Nicole Kidman

" The standard and quality of the stories are awe-inspiring. They are poignant, moving and some extremely heartfelt. My congratulations to all the finalists. **"**

   – Jim Broadbent

" The incredible talent on display in these stories is truly impressive. This genuinely moving and authentic writing is a much needed rallying cry for change. "

   – Mark Strong

" I was so moved by the range of skilful, moving stories featured in 500 Words: Black Lives Matter. These are some seriously talented young writers. "

   – Colin Jackson

PRAISE FOR 500 WORDS: BLACK LIVES MATTER

" Poignant, incredibly assured and deeply emotional storytelling. Their brilliant response to why Black Lives Matter, is an exemplary model for empathy, compassion and understanding of the world we live in. I have been blown away by the quality and skill of these young writers. "

— Shobna Gulati

" In a time of such bleak uncertainty, these gifted and sensitive young writers give great hope for the future. I encourage them all to keep writing and using their talent. "

— Rob Brydon

" Our future feels in good hands with these phenomenal, powerful stories. I found them genuinely moving, thought provoking and they gave me such hope. What a wonderful and inspiring project to be involved in and what incredible future screenwriters, novelists, authors and warriors we have in waiting for the years to come. Such a joyful and important creative endeavour beautifully carried out. "

– Amanda Abbington

" I think the 500 words competition this year focussing on the Black Lives Matter movement is a wonderful way to get young children to learn and understand about the importance of equality. It allows children to be creative and describe their feelings and this is so important for their mental health. "

– Joe Wicks

THE HEAD JUDGES

There were almost 6,000 stories submitted to 500 Words: Black Lives Matter! A team of public judges, made up of teachers and librarians read and marked all the entries. The top 2,500 stories were professionally read by The Reading Agency who suggested the top sixteen entries to the judging panel.

The judging panel, consisting of Angellica Bell, Michael Underwood and head judges Malorie Blackman, Frank Cottrell-Boyce, Francesca Simon and Charlie Higson chose the top eight stories, and from those one winner in each age category.

Malorie Blackman

Former children's laureate and author of over 60 books Malorie Blackman is best known for her YA book series "Noughts & Crosses".

Frank Cottrell-Boyce

Carnegie medal winner Frank Cottrell-Boyce is the author of many critically-acclaimed children's books including *Sputnik's Guide to Life*.

Francesca Simon

Creator of "Horrid Henry", Francesca Simon is the author of over 50 books — one of her stories *The Monstrous Child* was even turned into an opera!

Charlie Higson

Screenwriter, actor and children's author Charlie Higson is best known as the author of the "Young Bond" and "Enemy" book series.

5-9
YEARS

PRAISE FOR THE WINNERS

WINNER: I FEEL OUT OF CONTROL!
Sara De Jong

Of the winning story the judges said:
"This is a real gem of a story and is deeply, deeply rooted in reality.
The last sentence is one of the best closes I've ever read."
 — *Malorie Blackman*

"Easily and by far the most accomplished piece of work in this category,
a joy to read."
 — *Frank Cottrell-Boyce*

"Well done, your story is sensational! Whilst it read like an essay it
created an engaging and amazing story."
 — *Francesca Simon*

"Of all the stories we've read, this remained with me for a long time.
It's incredibly memorable and is such an important piece of writing."
 — *Charlie Higson*

FINALIST: Something You're Not
Katherine Ebrey

What the judges said:
"What a beautiful story. It encourages all of us to embrace who we are rather than something we're not."
— *Malorie Blackman*

"The narrative encourages us to find the space where we belong and enjoy what connects us."
— *Frank Cottrell-Boyce*

"A wonderful story that explores the importance of seeing beyond superficial difference."
— *Francesca Simon*

"What a delightful and thought provoking read."
— *Charlie Higson*

PRAISE FOR THE WINNERS

FINALIST: Grandpa is
Emerson Nwaneri

What the judges said:
"There's a sweet use of language in this and it pays homage to Grandpa beautifully."
— *Malorie Blackman*

"I really enjoyed the alternative take you took, it's imaginative and creative."
— *Frank Cottrell-Boyce*

"This really stayed with me, it's such a lovely personal piece."
— *Francesca Simon*

"The use of language is so simple, yet so effective and you approached it from a different angle."
— *Charlie Higson*

FINALIST: Love Is Colour-blind
Evie Bertin

What the judges said:
"I loved this lighter piece. It's refreshing and fun but carries a message."
— Malorie Blackman

"What an ambitious, inventive and bold piece."
— Frank Cottrell-Boyce

"The combination of humour with the serious topic is genius."
— Francesca Simon

"The last line is very funny, it made us all laugh and I think Boris would too if he heard it."
— Charlie Higson

WINNER:
I FEEL OUT OF CONTROL!
Sarah De Jong

George Floyd was killed in Minneapolis.

A police officer knelt on his neck until he died. George Floyd was black. The police officer is white. People are marching to demand that it does not happen again. They are marching against police cruelty, and against racism. I feel out of control: I'm so angry and sad. When I feel like this, I like to draw pictures. I find that it helps me to feel better. But today – today was different. I took my bucket of chalk and headed outside to start drawing on the sidewalk. I began writing George Floyd's name in big yellow letters when my neighbour Mohammed walked by.

"I'm angry, too," he said.

He picked up a piece of chalk and started drawing figures of the protesters inside my bubble letters. While Mohammed drew, he shared his own stories of racism. My classmate Ping walked by.

"I can't believe this happened," he said and, grabbing a piece of chalk, started drawing.

Ping explained how the discrimination he and his family face has gotten worse with COVID-19.

"I'm not a virus, you know," he said as he drew a large sunflower onto the sidewalk.

Mohammed and I nodded. "We know."

My neighbour Ana came by. Ana arrived in the UK some twenty years ago from Poland.

"This world has become very scary," she said as she bent down and made a summer sky with sweeps of blue and white chalk.

"Some people broke all the windows at my son's grocery shop because of Brexit and wrote 'Go Home' across the door," she finally whispered.

Mohammed patted her hand. Kwame, my best friend from next door, came over carrying a list of people's names who also faced police unkindness. He took a piece of chalk and began writing their names inside Ping's sunflower. Terrence Crutcher was killed by police, even though he had no gun and was no threat, Kwame explained as he signed his name to the sidewalk.

"Mr Crutcher's death led to protests in Tulsa. Eric Garner died after being placed in a strangling hold by a police officer. He died because he couldn't breathe – just like George Floyd," Kwame said quietly. "Breonna Taylor was shot by police while standing in her own apartment." Kwame wrote her name. "Freddie Gray died in the back of a police van. He broke his neck!" Kwame carefully added Gray's name.

Together, Mohammed, Ping, Ana, Kwame and I drew at the centre of our drawing a picture of George Floyd. I drew the head, while Ping drew the eyes and nose. Kwame drew the ears and mouth, Ana the hair and Mohammed the upper body. I proudly looked at the drawing we made. I knew that tonight's rain would likely wash away our drawing, and I knew that tomorrow morning I would likely wake up feeling again out of control and needing to draw. But for today, I said softly to myself, "I can breathe now."

RUNNER UP:
Something You're Not
Katherine Ebrey

WANTED: BLUE DRUMMER

Ruby read the banner. She felt a ripple of excitement; she knew this was her chance to finally be in a band. She took the banner home to her mum so she could see. Once she got home, she showed her mum. Her mum frowned and looked worried.

"But darling, you can't be in a blue band because you're a Red. You have red hair and they have blue. Don't try and be something you're not."

But Ruby took no notice. She went upstairs, got out her laptop and ordered a bottle of Super Sapphire hair dye. The next day, Ruby set off to the audition bright and early, with her freshly-dyed new blue hair flowing in the wind. On her name tag, instead of Ruby, it read Violet. The auditions were held in a big wood full of bluebells. Ruby felt the sun on her face as she bashed and crashed on the drum kit.

The leader of the band, Sinnika, smiled and cried out, "Way to go, Violet! We have to have you in our band."

Siyan and Indy nodded approval towards Ruby and they said, "You are a natural drummer, Violet!"

Ruby glowed with pride; she was going to be in the famous Blue Bashers band!

But then, all of a sudden, it started to pour with rain! Everyone rushed under the gazebo for shelter, but Ruby was lost in the music.

As she played, the rain trickled over her head onto her face and Sinnika cried out, "LOOK AT HER HAIR!"

Everyone turned to face Ruby. The hair dye was a puddle on the floor and, as they looked up, they saw her hair had got soaked and was as red as a cherry. Ruby stopped and realised what had happened. She froze in horror.

Siyan cried out, "What on earth happened to your – " he stopped – "RED hair?"

Ruby tried to speak, but no words came out. Her eyes welled up with tears and she ran from the woods, leaving a single drumstick behind in a puddle of blue dye. The Blue Bashers looked at each other.

Indy said, "She's got red hair. She's not like us at all." "But she is," said Sinnika. "She drums like we do. She gets lost in the music like us."

They all said in unison, "We've GOT to fix this."

The Blue Bashers picked up the drumstick and Indy fetched a new, clean sheet of paper. On it she wrote:

WE NEED OUR DRUMMER BACK!
WHETHER YOU ARE VIOLET OR NOT,
IF THIS STICK BELONGS TO YOU,
YOU ARE MEANT TO BE ONE OF US.
COME AND GET IT!

Days later, when Ruby read the new banner, her mouth twisted into a smile for the first time since the audition. She ran back to the woods to meet the Blue Bashers. But something had changed. Each and every band member now had a different colour hair.

"Welcome to the Rainbow Rockers," they shouted. "Let's play!"

RUNNER UP:
Grandpa is
Emerson Nwaneri

Grandpa is a fresh brown bun from the local shop
A treat of toast and tea in the morning just for we
Grandpa is helping around the house
Only the best will do for nan
Givin' her de favourite tomato soup in a pan
Grandpa is laughing at the telly telling jokes every night
Telling us about his stories that made us very bright
Grandpa is going shopping for us don't matter de price
Getting ice-cream and chocolate cake
Always treating us to something great
Grandpa is Jamaican style food
Loving de fried dumplin' and hot chicken
Always wanting us to go there with him
Grandpa says "mind yh don't fall down the stairs yh nah"
Grandpa is nice.

RUNNER UP:
Love is Colour-blind
Evie Bertin

Summer 2020 is over, and it turned out to be a horrible nightmare.

It all started with the prime minister Boris Johnson's shocking announcement on the evening news, "The World is fighting another pandemic, a new virus is spreading across the globe and is about to reach our country."

He tells us that it's nothing like we have ever seen before as the virus attacks our eyesight, so nobody will be able to see colours anymore. All colours have disappeared from our vision, like a sort of colour-blindness, so we can no longer tell each other apart. The Prime Minister has reassured us that our eyesight will come back in a few months when the pandemic is defeated or when a vaccine is invented.

People started to get ready for the virus to attack. Scientists worked around the clock to find a vaccine for this new threat. Communities started labelling the colour of their clothes, crayons, medicines, food, hot and cold taps, paints and pens so that they wouldn't mix the wrong colours together or put themselves in danger.

Two weeks later, Boris told the nation, "The virus is here so be prepared for what will happen. You can go about your everyday life but we now all look the same, so wear name badges, keep calm and carry on."

Meanwhile, the pandemic has spread around the world. The nations can no longer distinguish colours. For generations some people had been friends with people who only appeared like themselves and this had caused a lot of upset and inequality amongst others. So, with this colour blindness virus, we made new friends and were even enjoying the pandemic as it made us think more freely, and we were all treated as equals because we look the same as each other. Instead of judging people by the colour of their skin, we were seeing people for who they really are, their personality, kindness and if they made us laugh. People were supporting each other and sharing stories about their life and we started to feel much more united during the pandemic. We soon realised that in many ways we are all the same because deep down we are all human beings, and nothing changes just because of our skin colour or culture, but it is our personalities and things we like that makes us special.

Six months later, Boris appeared back on the TV in full colour and said, "The pandemic is over and we have found a vaccine, it will be delivered to your house at midday today, and soon we can all see colours again and everything will appear as it used to do."

When our vision returned to normal, we found we had made all sorts of new friends from different cultures and life was so much better and happier. Unfortunately for Boris, he had forgotten to label his clothes and appeared with blue hair, a pink suit, brown shirt and a doughnut tie.

The End.

White and Black, Cats and Mice
Lula Jankovic

It all started when the new family arrived in the village.

Things that had been simple before, suddenly felt complicated. You see, the cats didn't like it when the mouse family came. Everything had been perfect before. They knew their neighbours. They took care of their kittens. Life was simple.

As soon as the mice stepped foot in the village, everything was wrong. Suspicions were whispered. Rumours started. The mice were dangerous. The mice were crafty. The mice would steal. The mice were vermin. The mice would nibble and chew and destroy everything. House prices would never be the same again.

The mayor, his wife and children made a list of what mice weren't allowed to do. They displayed it at the Village Hall and pinned it on lamp posts. No mice allowed in Cat Shops – Mice cannot drive cars – Mice cannot buy houses - Mice cannot trespass on Cat property – Mice cannot jog in walking areas – Mice can only ride at the back of buses.

But one of the Mayor's children was concerned. Every day, she saw the little mice playing by the lane on her way to school. She didn't think it was fair for the mice. One afternoon on her way home, she bumped into one of the tiny mice.

"Hello," she said.

"Hi...," whispered the mouse shyly, looking at the ground.

"My name's Lettuce," said the kitten.

"I...I... I'm Amaria," answered the little mouse, cradling a minute doll made from twigs.

Lettuce looked at the fragile toy and thought of her huge playroom filled with balls and dolls and scratch towers.

"Why don't you come to school?" asked Lettuce.

"It's not allowed," said Amaria.

"But you're a child just like me. We are different that's all," said Amaria, straightening her cotton dress.

"It's always like this wherever we go."

The two girls walked down the lane together. Instead of going to her piano lesson, Lettuce visited the mouse family in their camper van. The camper van was cosy with bunks and bunting. Fairy lights hung above the table. Amaria's mother had lit candles and prepared a simple dinner.

"Don't you eat cheese?" asked Lettuce, looking at the rice and beans in her bowl. "I thought mice only ate cheese."

"There are lots of things that people think about us that aren't true," said Amaria.

"I've got an idea," said Lettuce. "Do you have any paints?" she asked.

The girls made banners: "Mice deserve an education too!"

The next day, they stood outside the village school before Assembly. Then, when the bell went, Lettuce took Amaria by the hand.

"You're coming with me," she said, and she marched into her classroom and sat down at her desk, pulling up a chair for her tiny friend.

Charlie's Special Formula
Samuel Clifford

Charlie Cloud is just a normal little boy with long curly hair and a great big smile.

He lives with his mum, dad and little brother Jack. His favourite thing to do is play football with his friends and family. He loves to watch TV and his favourite show is Deadly Sixty presented by Steve Backshall. Charlie loves going to school, his favourite subject is science and he loves to experiment. He also loves to see his friends. His best friend is Cristiano Ronaldo Junior!

His friends are all different. They have different hair colour, eye colour and skin colour. Although he had never really noticed that before. His gang is made up of girls and boys who all like different types of sport.

It is the summer of 2020 and the world has gone into lockdown because of the coronavirus. Charlie Cloud is annoyed and sad because he can't play football with his friends and he can't go to school because they are closed because of the deadly virus! Charlie has been at home for eleven weeks now, he goes to the park nearly every day and his mum and dad are at home more, although they watch the news aaaall the time!

Tonight, he heard something terrible: that a black man named George Floyd had been killed by police.

Charlie thought, "Who does that and why?"

After that there were big crowds called protests, everyone was so angry and wanted the world to change. Charlie Cloud started to think how he could help. He stayed up all night thinking about what he could do. All of a sudden, he realised science was the key, he would make a magic formula to give to grown-ups so they could see the world like children do with all people the same and no such thing as racism. Charlie decided his formula would be made of random things that babies, like only more revolting: mushy baby food, rotten baby milk and rusty rattle toys.

Charlie got straight to work creeping to his lab in the secret basement of his house. He put on his goggles and lab coat and he was ready to go! He put the ingredients in a "miniaturiser", stirred them in the pot and left it overnight to form – it smelt disgusting, Charlie hoped it would work. By the morning it was ready. Charlie decided to send the formula to Boris Johnson and it arrived within a minute.

Suddenly the time had come. Boris drank the formula and he sent it to all the adults.

The reviews are coming in now. Charlie is so nervous… it is a success! Charlie cannot believe it. He has made the world change forever for the better. Charlie Cloud will go down in history for reminding grown-ups how to see the world in a better way.

In The Court
Toluwa Teriba

The court was silent.

The policeman accused of three murders was sat silently in the centre of the room aware people were also watching his trial on TV. He also knew how he wanted this trial to end – with him found not guilty. He was almost arrogantly confident the mostly Caucasian jury would never find him guilty and his legal team also requested a particular judge who they believed could rule in their favour.

"You," boomed judge Jessica, "have murdered three people this year, is that right?"

"I…" stammered the scared policeman.

"Answer!" shouted the judge.

"My lawyer will in my defence explain how it all happened with all 3 people," he answered to the judge coldly.

"Mrs Mendstone," she said, hinting for the lawyer to talk in the policeman's defence. "My client, Mr Hautings committed these acts as a result of him trying to defend himself and the lives of others. A group of violent protesters attacked the police with clubs and my client had no option but to use his firearm to scare them back. Accidentally all 3 shots fired from his gun hit and killed 3 black protesters."

At this point, the prosecution lawyer jumped up and shouted, "Such a coincidence for you to have singled out and killed 3 black persons from the pack of protesters, sounds more like Mr Hautings specifically targeted and killed them because of their skin colour."

Judge Jessica had had enough of the shouting, turned to the jury, and announced that people who thought the man was innocent should raise their hands. Only thirteen from a fifty-man jury raised their hands.

"But…" started the policeman.

"Order!" interrupted Jessica, banging her gavel on the table. "And those who think he is guilty?" The rest of the jury raised their hands.

The opinion of the jury was a very clear decision. The judge went into a quick recess and came back with a twenty-five years prison sentence. Mr Hautings dropped his head in disappointment, he showed no emotion or offered any apology to the families of the dead people. The court security placed him in handcuffs, and he was taken away.

"Cut!" ordered the film director. "Good shoot everyone. We can take a quick break, relax for some minutes, and have some smoothie."

All of the actors poured off of the stage and took a seat at the smoothie bar to discuss their parts in the movie.

"I quite enjoyed my part," said the man who played Mr.Hautings while catching up with Jessica, who is a retired judge and just trying out a new career in acting. "I normally act nicer roles in the other movies I have been in"

"This scene actually uses my experience as a judge. I also enjoyed the sentencing as I believe it sends out a strong message that black lives matter. I'm excited about our next project and I think it will send another message."

Once they had finished their break, they went back to the stage and began another scene.

The King and the Cake
Matilda Rua

Once there was the Kingdom of the Blue Sea.

It was ruled by a good king, he loved people from the close by villages to come and stay in his town. He welcomed people from the kingdoms of the Yellow Desert, Pink Strawberries, Green Jungle and many more.

One day the good king died, and his evil brother called Greedy Geoff took over. He was called greedy because he spent all day eating cakes and sweets in fact, he was very big. Greedy Geoff didn't like that people from different kingdoms could mix, he thought that the Blue-Sea people were better than anyone else.

So, he divided the kingdom and built some walls to separate the town. From that day people were not allowed to mix, go to the same schools, use the same buses, shop in same supermarket or even use the same toilets!! The Blue people had the fanciest houses while the Yellows, Pinks and the Greens had very little space. Only the Blues were happy, everyone else was feeling miserable.

In the Blue neighbourhood there was a little girl called Lucy, she was missing her friends a lot. Lucy wanted to visit her friend Sophia from the Pink Strawberries. She stopped at her cottage. There was a beautiful smell coming out of the window. When she opened the door, she saw a cake, it looked fabulous.

"Yum this cake looks delicious," cried Lucy.

"Yes, me and my mum are baking it when I miss my village, the ingredients are from my hometown," explained Sophia.

Lucy and Sophia secretly started visiting all of their friends. Often there were lots of delicious cakes made with ingredients from all-over. Meanwhile Greedy Geoff was fed up having to eat the same cakes every day. He wanted something different, so he decided to host a cake competition, and of course only the blue people were allowed to take part.

Lucy had a brave plan.

She secretly met all of her friends and baked a cake with many different ingredients from all the kingdoms. It took 5 months, but finally the cake was ready! It tasted gloriously good! They called it the Rainbow Cake.

When the king tasted it his face lit up. "This cake is

wonderful!! What is your name little girl? Why is this cake so good?!"

"My name is Lucy. I made the cake with all my friends from the different neighbourhoods mixing their home-town ingredients!"

A little tear rolled down the king's cheek. He understood that everything he had done was wrong. That day the walls between the neighbourhoods got knocked down, and finally the king declared that all the people could mix again! Everyone was happy and they had a big celebration. There was music, food and dancing. The king was wiggling his chubby bottom!

Everybody was up all-night partying. Lucy was very pleased that the king understood that everybody is important, because it does not matter what you look like on the outside, it is the inside that counts.

Year 2
Beatrice Martin

Portsmouth grammar school. Year 2 has arrived!

I zoom to my classroom and await the surprise! Who will I meet? Where will I play? The possibilities are infinite on my very first day.

Dr Habib catches my eye. Her smile is contagious, and I wonder why does she wear a headscarf full of sparkling jewels? She looks like a princess, born to rule!

Cenaru is waiting for me by his desk. He is cheeky and funny, my friend is the best! We clasp hands and spin round in a bubble of joy. It's brilliant to be back at school with this boy.

Eloisa is beautiful, beside her I feel plain. Her family are all from a small village in Spain. She greets me with two kisses, one on each cheek. I love her warm "Hola!"

She is truly unique.

Addison wears her traditional robes with long dangling earrings, 3 in each lobe! She dazzles in bright colours and her sweetness we love most. Her mum cooks gorgeous recipes from the Caribbean coast.

Then there is me, a total mixed dish half Indian, quarter Italian and quarter English! I enjoy people guessing my ancestral list. It's brilliant being British with a cultural twist.

This is our class – our glorious year 2! We are all 6 or 7 and all have our views. Our heritage comes from far and from wide. We are multiracial and proud with nothing to hide. We see the world rainbow. A fuse of traditions of race and unity will ultimately be our generation's greatest mission. We view all our classmates with mutual respect. Why haven't our adults caught on to this yet? Year 2 will be the pioneers. The more we talk about it the more people will hear. Infants are great at talking, Year 2's probably the most. I hope when I'm a junior, these views I can still boast!

Friends Forever
Amelia Turnbull

Two girls are the very best of friends.

They did everything together in school and sat next to each other in class. Harleen helped Izzy with spellings while Izzy helped Harleen with maths sums, and in art class they painted portraits of each other. Break-time was their favourite time of day, with hopscotch, skipping, basketball, doing each other's hair and making memories full of fun and giggling.

Things were fantastic, that is until home time.

Their parents didn't understand Harleen and Izzy's friendship. They couldn't see how close they were or why they had painted a portrait with the wrong colour skin and hair. The girls loved their differences and enjoyed celebrating their own cultures with each other, dressing up in amazing clothes and learning to dance or being shown the best way to get all of the yucky stuff out of a pumpkin.

Izzy's parents decided that they didn't like this and moved Izzy to a new school away from her best friend.

The girls couldn't understand why their families didn't understand or why they had been torn apart from one another, a precious friendship now with two broken hearts.

Going to school was no longer fun, Harleen looked at the empty seat next to her on a school trip and felt all alone. She opened her bag and pulled out the portrait of Izzy, her tears streamed down her cheeks uncontrollably. Other kids called her names for this. It just made Harleen feel even more sad and alone.

Izzy felt lost at her new school. She had no one to help her with her spellings, to play with or sit talking non-stop to. She was alone too, with thoughts of her best friend. As they grew the girls never forgot their special friendship. Starting secondary school was as scary as moving schools for Izzy.

As she looked at the map to find her next class, she accidently bumped into another student. While muttering a nervous apology, she looked up to see two big brown eyes that she'd know anywhere stared back at her. The girls stopped, people from every direction buzzed around them but they couldn't move. After all of this time, they had found each other again. In an instant they were jumping up and down hugging each other. Realising they had to get to class they checked the timetable and found that they were in the same lesson, sitting next to each other once again. Things were perfect. Break was back to talking non-stop. They had lots to catch up on.

The girls are grown-ups now and still best friends with children of their own who are still always there for each other but instead of spellings and maths they help each other with their children and juggling life. They still make time for their catch ups where they talk non-stop and fill time with laughter. And each had a very old portrait framed in their homes. The forever friends. Changing attitudes together.

Black Panther's Journey
Maxim Abbas

Long ago, there once lived a friendly Panther.

He had little jaws, green eyes that glowed like a lightning bolt and beautiful, shiny black fur. When Panther was 4 years old, he was lonely. He wished he had some friends to play with and went on a journey to make some.

First, he bumped into Flamingo. Flamingo was a colourful pink and looked strong and friendly. Panther decided to say hello.

"Hi, my name is Panther. I came from a faraway place and I'm looking for friends"

Flamingo was scared!

"Sorry we can't be friends! Your black fur is scary," and she scattered away.

Panther was shocked and sad, but he didn't give up. He soon met a bright and colourful parrot.

"Hello, my name is Panther. I came from far away and I'm looking for friends."

Parrot was flapping through the sky and in a rather

sticky voice said, "I am colourful and beautiful, I can't be friends with you. Look at your black fur. I don't want to be friends with you," Parrot scrambled and flew away.

Panther was sad. "It's just fur, what's wrong? It shouldn't matter." He still wouldn't give up, so he continued his journey when he met a tiny tree frog.

"What are you doing here?" said the frog.

"Hello, I'm Panther. I've come from far away and I'm looking for friends. Flamingo ran away and Parrot said she wouldn't play with me because of my black fur. That made me sad. I am an animal of the jungle, just like you."

"Why should we be friends with you? We're colourful and we need colourful friends!" Tree frog jumped away.

Panther felt like giving up when he took his final chance on one more animal. Emerging from a dark bush came Chamelion. Chameleon was the wisest animal of the jungle.

"Hello, my name in Chameleon. I've been watching you this whole time. I've followed your journey, in camouflage. I feel sad and sorry for you. I shall call my friends from the jungle."

Chameleon gathered all the animals.

"I've called you here because it doesn't matter what

colour we are. I am sad with you all for being rude to Panther. All he wanted was a friend," he said. "Panther, I am sorry for how you were treated. I would like to invite you to a party with all the animals to say sorry. It doesn't matter if we have different colours. It doesn't matter if we have fur or skin or feathers. What matters is being kind and smiley and friendly and funny."

The animals were sad with themselves. They promised not to choose friends for their colour again. They said sorry to Panther and had the best party ever! The jungle animals of all colours are now friends. Black Lives Matter.

The end.

Black Wasps Matter
Erin Bateson

A long time ago Bees and Wasps lived in harmony, flying amongst the flowers and racing through the grass.

But one day, something changed.

The Bees built hives and the Wasps got left behind. Bees got the best jobs, making honey for the queen, they got their pick of the best flowers, they grew fat whilst the Wasps grew weary. When Bees were thirsty humans gave them water to drink and a place to sit and rest. When a Wasp flew by the same home, the children screamed in fear and the mum chased it with a rolled-up newspaper threatening to kill it. Bees were deemed cute and cuddly, Wasps were viewed as ugly, nasty pests. They were the same in so many ways but treated so differently.

Walter was a young Wasp. He grew up in a predominantly bee-populated area. All his classmates were Bees and he never realised there was any difference between him and his friends until one difficult day when a child got stung. Walter's best friend was a Bee named

Beatrice. Walter and Beatrice were inseparable – they did everything together. Beatrice would show Walter the best flowers and in turn Walter would give Beatrice flying lessons.

One day, a group of friends visited a park in the neighbouring village. Little did they know that this trip would change everything between them. When they got to the park there were many wildflowers that Walter had never seen before, Beatrice flew among them, sharing her knowledge with Walter who was fascinated. She was just explaining the inner workings of a cornflower when a shadowy figure appeared. It was an evil little boy, and, in a flash, he had trapped Beatrice in a glass.

"Got one," he shouted in excitement, running back to his group of friends on the other side of the park. Walter raised the alarm with the other Bees and being the fastest flyer, chased the boy and Beatrice.

"Pull its wings off," one member of the nasty pack shouted.

"No, squash it!" said another.

Seeing his friend in such peril, sparked something. in Walter – a sense of anger took over his body. Without thinking, he flew at the boy and stung him. The child dropped the glass and Beatrice flew out. At that moment the rest of the Bees arrived, just in time to see the boy rolling around in pain.

"Walter, how could you?!?" they cried.

Walter tried to explain himself but who would believe a poor old Wasp? The Bees had already decided what had happened. This was just another example of an angry young Wasp crossing the line. All the way home, Walter tried to tell them what had really happened, but no one wanted to listen. Walter's mum sobbed. She had tried so hard to make peace with the Bees but now she must choose between supporting her son or keeping things sweet with the Bee community who wanted Walter sent to prison.

The Rainbow
Hareem Zaidi

You know, the rainbow wasn't always the rainbow.

Once, a long time ago, the colours were separated. They always used to fight because they were different, and they fought so much that they even had boundaries for each colour: red, orange, yellow, green, blue and purple. Each strip of colour had to stay in those boundaries – they were not allowed to cross to another colour, it's not like they wanted to anyway.

However, there was a strip of purple who was very curious, and she always used to sit just behind the purple boundary between the blues and stare and wonder about this mysterious other side. One day, a strip of blue saw this strip of purple but, instead of telling her to go away, he sat there with her, and they began to talk.

Ever since then, they used to wake up really early in the morning every day, and just chat and chat and chat and chat. I'm sure you get the idea! They became the best of friends, but of course, they had to keep this a secret from the others. Over the years, they fell in love and had a baby called indigo. She was like blue and purple mixed up together. She was beautiful and like nothing they had ever seen before.

Somehow, one day, purple's sister found out about all of this and told all the blues and purples. Both blues and purples were absolutely FURIOUS! The blues told blue to come back, and the purples told purple to come back, and if they didn't, they would be called BETRAYERS, and everyone would make fun of their families and them! Blue and purple didn't want to let their families down, so they did.

Then indigo came and cried, "Oh mummy, daddy you have to be together, who will look after me?" Everybody's hearts melted.

They felt sorry for the little one and said "Don't worry, mummy and daddy are here for you. They will always be together."

Indigo was over the moon. The purples and blues had a little chat and decided that they wanted to take down their boundary, but of course, they would have to have permission from the others. So, the purples and blues marched along confidently to the other side and demanded that the other colours should break down all the boundaries.

"OK, we DO NOT care!" red, orange, yellow and green replied, not even bothered.

So, all the colours just decided that only the blue and purple boundary would break. The blues and purples were overjoyed, and the greens saw how much fun it looked. So, the greens gathered all of their confidence then went over to the blues and purples.

They shyly asked, "Can we join you? It's just that it looks so fun and—"

"Of course you can!" purple and blue replied, excited for another colour to join them.

After that, all the colours slowly, but surely became friends. And they made, what we call today, the rainbow.

The Greatest Gymnast
Sofie Britto

"In the code of points, difficulty is very valued now. Of course, this suits African Americans. They're very explosive – look at the NBA, who's playing and jumping there?"

Simone's heart thumped as these words replayed in her mind. Her mind. A mind taught to be strong and fearless. Why did her mind capture these bad words so helplessly? Stabbing and chipping away at her strength like a chisel to stone. These bad words, spoken and quoted by US Coordinator Valeri Luikin recently, brought a sense of injustice and humiliation with it; not just to Simone, but to all people of colour who work hard.

"It's my hard work that's brought me to where I am today. Not my African American physique," Simone hissed under her breath as she took two steps forward towards the large blue industrial mat.

She noticed it had more powder on it than usual, reminding her of her childhood in Ohio, Texas. How she giggled gleefully whilst galloping into her mamma's arms on the first day of that magical snowfall. Mamma, sitting on the first bench, in between her Coach and Pappa. Mamma's hair looked frizzy today. It glinted through the light reflecting off the Beams and strangely, matched the leotards of Team Russia. Black and shiny with silver sequins. Catching Mamma's eye, Simone's breathing slowed down as Mamma mouthed lovingly, "My Baby, go get 'em."

A sharp crackle pierced the stuffiness of the stadium and the crowd quietened down, shocked from the echo of the microphone which was struggling to push the commentator's voice through.

"Ayynd, reprezenin the US of A, Simone Biles. Five times gold medallist, right he-yer in Tokyo tweny tweny. No need for introductions. The whole world knows about her; the girl who flaaaaiis." Throats were cleared and a few people sniffed nervously.

Now was the time to show supporters in the stadium and millions worldwide, that Simone Biles deserved her sixth gold. But her legs felt like lead, her arms like planks of wood and her mind foggy with Valeri's bad words. Did others agree with Valeri? Were they here in the crowd? At home on their sofas, looking at Simone's body and analysing every inch of her? Believing her success was down to her genetics alone? This was a fight Simone had to battle every time she stepped onto that large blue mat or took on the Beams. The same fight many people of colour have to fight each and every day. The match was between Biting Bad words and inner strength. Each time, Simone Biles put herself forward for the match, she did just what Mamma taught her to do: "Do your BEST."

With head held high, eyes focussed and limbs strong, Simone took charge of that mat. With each record-breaking turn, flip and somersault, she claimed her rightful place. The crowds gasped with delight and cheered frantically at her triple somersault back flip. The glory was all hers. Simone Biles. The girl who dared to "Fly to the Sky".

Black and White
Gracie Salter

"Sit down, class," cried Mrs Williams as a flock of children flowed in.

"Today we are learning history."

"BORING!" shouted Maisy.

"But it's the way we are doing it." Mrs Williams pulled out a peculiar knick-knack from her pocket. "GRAB ON!" she screamed.

"AAAAAAAAAAAAAAAAAAHHHHHHHHHHH HHHHHHHHHHHHHH"

The knick-knack was a time machine. "This is Harriot. She lived just over one hundred years ago. She was a heroine, she freed slaves from farms."

"Miss, slaves were in the Roman times," said Trixie. "Well…"

Mrs Williams looked away. "GRAB ON!"

"AAAAAAAAAAAAAAAAAAHHHHHHHHHHH HHHHHHHHHHHHHH"

"This is Rosa, she sat on a bus in 1955 in America

and still got in trouble."

"You must mean spitting not sitting?" asked Josh.

"Mmm…" Mrs Williams looked away again. "GRAB ON!"

"AAAAAAAAAAAAAAAAAAHHHHHHHHHHH HHHHHHHHHHHHHHH"

"This is Martin. He was shot in 1968 because he had a dream that one day black and white children would be treated the same."

"That didn't really happen did it Mrs?" said Ben.

"Errr….". Mrs Williams looked away. "GRAB ON!"

"AAAAAAAAAAAAAAAAAAAAAAAAAAAAA HHHHHHHHHHHHHHHH"

"This is Mary. She struggled to get a job as a nurse, even though she was great."

"But Miss, everyone needs nurses, why would they refuse a great one?" said Daisy.

"It's not always like that," said Mrs Williams. "GRAB ON!"

"AAAAAAAAAAAAAAAAAHHHHHHHHHHH HHHHHHHHHHHHH"

"This is present day. People still aren't treated the same."

Everyone looked over and saw a tramp sitting on a bench.

"Anyone have some food for him?" said Mrs Williams.

"I do Miss," said Torben. "It's a granola bar."

"OK," said Mrs Williams. "Can you give it to him?"

Torben crept over nervously and gave him the granola bar. He scoffed it down like he'd never seen food before.

"Thank you," he said with a glisten in his eyes.

"How did you become a tramp?" asked Torben.

"My country is in a big war," he said. He spoke in an African voice. He wasn't fluent in English yet.

"My family's in jail." He was starting to cry a bit.

"Don't worry we will HELP!" bellowed the whole class.

"We could start a campaign…" "We could do a bake sale…" "We—"

"Guys stop. What we need to do is tell people how unfair it all is and always has been," said Torben.

"Torben is right," said the tramp.

[2 minutes later on the high street]

"Hello mam, we—"

"Not interested."

[2 HOURS later back at the bench]

No luck.

"Children, you're kind and helpful. Your teacher is right to show you a bit of history. Everything you do now will make a difference."

Just as the class started to leave, Mrs Williams fell and hurt her leg.

"I'll help her," said the tramp. "I used to be a doctor but haven't found any work since I arrived here." So, he gave first aid and she was back on her feet in no time.

"Who was that?" questioned Tassy.

"Time to head back to class," said Mrs Williams, looking away. "GRAB ON!"

"AAAAAAAAAAAAAAAAAAAAAAAAAAAAAAAAA HHHHHHHHHHHHHHHHH"

"Miss, was that history lesson true?" asked Nyla.

"You decide." Mrs Williams looked away.

Black Lives Matter

Geovanni Lucianno Virimayi Nhemachena

Black Lives Matter.

As far back as 1619, without their consent, great people of Africa departed their continent, chained and forced into ships. Transported into foreign lands, black lives didn't matter then.

Made to work endless days and nights in cotton fields, given foreign names and robbed of their identity. Separated from their families, black lives didn't matter then.

Sold off to the highest bidders. People bidding like they were objects, black lives didn't matter then.

Forced to live in poor neighbourhoods, deprived of education, deprived of good health. Deprived of opportunities to prosper, black lives didn't matter then.

Great men and women finally rally, rallying and crying out for change, change of people's minds, change of policies. Black lives do matter. Great men like Martin Luther King, Great men like Nelson Mandela. Many others before and after them, all cry out for change, change of policies, change of people's minds. Will black lives now matter?

Still, police brutality rages on, stop and chase with no cause rages on. Singled out for the colour of your skin, I see rage on people's faces. Anger and cruelty, black lives seem not to matter.

Biased judiciary system, rigged from the word go, rigged against people of colour, black lives don't seem to matter. Mothers raising fatherless children, fathers killed in police custody, teenagers arrested for being suspicious looking. Suspicious because they are black or brown, black lives still don't seem to matter.

Derogatory names being uttered, compared to animals. Being treated far worse than animals, black lives don't seem to matter to them. Protesters grouping asking for change, being likened to terrorists for asking for change, being threatened to be shot or finally crying out for change, will anything ever change? Will black lives ever matter?

Single mothers wait on the doorstep, waiting for their black sons to come back home. No one is coming back home, because police have placed a knee on their necks. Black lives don't matter to them. A man cries out in pain, shouts out his mother's name, pleads for water but receives pain. Pleads to breathe but the knee keeps pressing, stares right into death's eyes, the knee keeps pressing, breathless and lifeless the man gives up, still a knee keeps pressing. Will black lives ever matter?

We shall protest until the end of time. Until black people in this world get the same rights as anyone else, there will be no peace. How can you sleep at night? How do you go on? Knowing fully well that one group is seen as superior than the other. Do black lives matter at all, I wonder?

Journey to Joy!
Olivia Simmons

Hi, I'm Lola and I come from the wonderful land of Jamaica.

I live in a small cosy beach hut that nestles neatly at the edge of our beautiful beach. I call it silky sands beach because of how it feels when I run through the golden granules. We spend our days playing on the silky sands, making fantastical toys from the clever coconut shells we collect. We give them names and my favourite is Colin the coconut, he was so kind sharing his sweet milk from inside. As I watch the sun set at the end of the day against the silvery sea, I think that my Jamaica is a little bit of heaven here on Earth and it makes me so happy and excited to start each day here. But we are leaving soon, going far away to a land called England.

When Daddy came back from the war, he told us we needed to go, that we needed to bring some sunshine to their sad and sorry land. Salty slithers of tears trickled down my face as I stamped my feet and said that I didn't want to go. But go we must and so, we left our little patch

of heaven and boarded a great white ship called the SS
Empire Windrush with towering decks as high as the sky.

I was scared and excited, but Daddy gave me a new
travelling companion whose cuddles made it all better. His
name is Bear, like a big brown bear with fur as soft as silk
and a smile so sweet it makes everything better. I told him
all about the adventures we would have and as he looked at
me with his raggedy face, I knew he understood how I felt.

We slept in a small cosy cabin deep down in the ship
and as the sea rolled, we travelled far beyond any horizon
I had ever seen. The voyage was long but lovely as it lolled
and lazed to the sound of the calypso music that played on
deck bringing a little bit of the Caribbean feeling with us.

We arrived at the dull and dreary dock. We put on
our Sunday best and tied ruby red ribbons in my hair ready
to be welcomed with opened arms. But there were no
open arms, there was no welcome. Daddy smiled and told
us not to be scared. So, we tiptoed around our Empire and
we knocked on door after door and we were met with
such strange words, "NO BLACK HERE!"

I didn't understand. Why weren't we wanted? Why
did they look at us like that? As time went on, we found
our way and brought our Caribbean dream to our little

home. But there is one wound that still remains and that Black lives Don't Matter. They Do! They did then and they do today, shout it loud and shout it proud for me Lola aged 9 and all our Windrush family.

Pigeon and Black Lives Matter
Caiden Geens

I am a pigeon and I live on a statue. I have been very happy living here for a long time, but things are different now.

It was a month ago when I heard something rattling. I flew up from my statue to see what it was, but I couldn't see anything. I could hear people chanting and shouting a long way away and the bottle what was on the statue fell off and cracked on the floor. I flew up to the building and flew in a gap in the building. From there I could see lots of black and white men and women. They were holding signs that said, "do not kill us" and "black lives matter". They were shouting at the air and at everyone and moving towards me. I flew over to get a closer look. There were grown-ups and children, they looked angry and they were reading their signs and saying the messages. It looked like it was really important. They were wearing face masks so they could stay one metre instead of two and it was a crazy crowd but if you put a measuring tape down you would see they were at least one metre apart. The crowd were walking quickly so I flew slowly across their heads and went back towards my statue.

They were getting closer and closer. Then I thought they were following me.

They marched up to my statue and I flew up to get away. Three of the group got a rope and climbed up and put it on the statue quickly and pulled and pulled, but it didn't move. They didn't stop. They kept tugging and tugging but it still didn't come down. Lots more people were pushing and tugging and lifting and after all of that the statue got flipped over on to the floor.

I couldn't believe what I was watching. I felt so sad that they had done this. My home!

I shouted but they didn't hear me because it was too noisy. The people cheered and shouted we did it! They were very happy and were rolling and rolling the statue to the river. For a while I was really sad. But now I realise that they did it for one reason. He was a mean white person, what gives everyone money but kept black people as slaves. It is a bad thing to do and we know that now. I have a new home now. I live in a building in the roof. I can see through the hole all the people being kind to each other and that is making me happy.

Billy's Mum's Birthday
Ruaridh Thorburn

Billy had been excited for weeks thinking about his mum's upcoming birthday. He had been saving up money to buy her a special present.

Every Saturday and Sunday afternoon he had been washing cars and cutting the neighbour's grass. One day walking home from school he had seen a beautiful necklace in the window display of the local jewellery store. It was silver with a shining blue cross pendant. This would be a perfect for his mum whose favourite colour was blue!

Every day she worked hard to keep their family going. That afternoon when he arrived home, he threw off his coat and backpack and sprinted up to his bedroom. He carefully tipped out his piggy bank and counted £20. He had enough to buy the pretty necklace!

That Friday after school he hurried to the jewellery shop and found the necklace hadn't been bought. He saw the shopkeeper helping another customer, so he decided to look at the shiny necklace. He picked it up and was so entranced by it, sparkling in the light like a glowing star. Suddenly, a firm hand grabbed him by the shoulder and spun him around.

"You are stealing," boomed the shopkeeper. "I am going to call the policeman. Look, I can see one walking up the road right now!"

"I was going to buy it," stammered Billy.

But the man wouldn't listen.

Then he walked to the door and shouted, "Policeman there is a thief in my shop!"

A tall strong-looking policeman entered through the door of the store.

"What's going on here?" he asked in a stern voice.

"This boy tried to steal from my shop, but I caught him red handed!"

"I was going to buy it for my mum," interrupted Billy and took out his £20 note to show the policeman.

"If he was going to steal it he would quickly put it in his pocket," said the policeman matter-of-factly. "Have you heard of the Black Lives Matter campaign? Everybody should be kinder towards each other and not so prejudiced."

Billy was so embarrassed that he just wanted to

leave. He didn't care about the necklace anymore.

The policeman said in a kind tone, "You can leave now I will sort this out."

Billy ran out the door quickly, crying as he sped off. Tears dropped to the ground like rain. When he arrived back, he told his mum everything that had happened.

"Don't worry about not buying the necklace, I love you so much Billy. We can go to the funfair that is in the town tomorrow and you can go on all the rides."

Billy's mum had the best birthday ever! They spent Billy's £20 on popcorn, hot dogs and lots of scary rides. The best was the Spinning Spider and they laughed all the way home.

Black Lives Matter
Jamie Thompson

Black Lives Matter.

It was a hot day in New York, 76 Fahrenheit. Fred Johnson was driving his police car, he was suspicious. He passed other cars, the police department, tall hotels and ranks of yellow taxis. He went down 34th Street. He took a drink of refreshing, cold water.

He drove past a black Lamborghini with a black person driving and thought he saw a weapon in the back seat. A sword. He saw the sun flash off the blade through the window. He was not sure if the heat was making him imagine it.

He followed the car. He was losing the car in the traffic, so he put his siren on and caught up with the car again but did not get too close, just in case the black man had a gun. The man parked outside a hotel and went in. Fred went to look into the back seat of the Lamborghini to see if there was really a sword. There was no sword. He took the registration number of the car. Fred had decided he wanted to question the man. The man was black so Fred thought he might have another weapon. Fred waited, then went into and searched the hotel from top to bottom. When he could not find the man, he went back outside and realised the car had left the parking lot.

Now he was on the hunt for this person. He had a hunch, so the first place he looked was at the airport. Fred thought the man might be trying to leave the country because he knew that Fred was after him. Fred searched the departure gates. The man was nowhere to be found. Fred used his walkie talkie to ask for a check on the car registration and was given an address. He was also given a name, Richie Fowler. Fred went to the house at the address.

The house was colourful, painted red and white. The Lamborghini was parked outside. The door was open. Fred went in to look for the man, it was cool inside out of the sun. He searched the kitchen. There were some knives. He was scared, the man might have a weapon. He searched the rest of downstairs, in all the hiding places but could not find anything of interest. Fred went upstairs and looked in the bathroom. Nothing. Fred went to the bedroom and he saw the man hiding under the bed.

He shouted, "Do you have a weapon?"

The man said, "I'm not going to answer that."

Fred was angry that the man did not answer so Fred shot him once. The bullet killed Richie Fowler, passing straight through his heart. Afterwards, when he checked the body, Fred realised the man did not have a weapon. He went outside and it was raining. People were standing outside. They were scared about what might have just happened to Richie. Fred heard one of them say "Black lives matter".

The protesting had only just started.

The Same Wrinkly Fingers and Toes
Evadne Kelly

In August 2018, when I was seven years old, I went on an amazing holiday with my mum and dad to Barbados.

My mum and dad are great, but they don't always want to play in the swimming pool with me and so sometimes on holiday I can get a bit bored of playing on my own.

I was in the pool playing when a girl turned up and said to me, "Would you like to play with me?" I did want to play, so I said yes.

We started playing straight away. In fact, we spent the next nine hours playing in the pool. We didn't want the day to end because we were having so much fun. When we got out of the pool, we both had the same wrinkly fingers and toes, we had been in the water for so long.

Alyssa and I like the same things, we can swim the same, we like to play the same games and we like the same food (we love KFC!). While we were playing in the pool, my parents were talking to Alyssa's dad and they liked the same things too. The next day, we played again. Alyssa was really interested in my hair and how different to hers it is, she wanted to touch it so I said she could. I loved her hair as well, so I asked if I could I feel her hair and she said yes. I love her hair because she has lots and lots of braids in, and when she goes in the water and comes out, her braids are not wet. Later, we went back in the pool and she put her swimming cap on and then it broke. So, we put it on our feet and started playing mermaids.

We played every day until Alyssa had to leave. On the day she had to leave we tried to get each other's contacts, but we could not get them because we did not know our contacts, so our dads swapped details and they speak all the time now too!

We hope to go and visit one day so we can play mermaids in the pool again. But until then, we can speak to each other on Zoom and WhatsApp. I hope we will always be friends. Her skin is a different colour to mine and her hair is a different texture but that does not matter to me. It does not matter to me because I like the person she is on the inside, Alyssa is funny, kind, beautiful, caring and she is a great swimmer. We are still friends now even though Barbados is her home and the UK is mine we speak on

Zoom or Facetime. I showed her the snow in our garden last winter and I even went to her virtual tenth birthday party this year.

A Birthday Surprise
Abigail Jackson

Tuesday 14th March 2016.

Dear Diary,

Firstly, before I tell you all about myself, I want to tell you what happened when I first saw you.

This morning, I was confused why my little sister Zuri was not wailing to be picked up, and why my older sister Jabali was asking me to do her make-up (everybody says I do make-up well). Then, I realised it was my birthday!

I excitedly changed into my birthday dress and ran downstairs which was lined with balloons and a huge banner that said: HAPPY BIRTHDAY AMANI! When I saw it, a huge smile appeared on my face because I was so happy. Then, when I thought things couldn't get better, they did. Because when I opened the first present, I saw you for the first time. It was like she dropped a bomb on my head, I thought she was joking or pretending so I played along.

"Where in England are we going?!" I asked.

"Hampshire," replied my mum.

Immediately all elatedness disappeared because I heard stories about that place, and they weren't particularly good. I'm Kenyan. I heard it was cold even for those who lived there. After that we went on many trips around Nairobi doing and buying things I've only ever dreamed of. But due to the England bombshell I wasn't able to enjoy the pleasures of my shopping spree.

Yours,

Amani.

Wednesday, 15th March 2016.

Dear Diary,

I tried everything, but it did not work. Honestly, I tried rolling around screaming that I wouldn't go. I tried begging and pretending I had amnesia so I couldn't recognise my parents anymore. I even had the audacity to sleepwalk so that my parents wouldn't dare trust me on the plane. But they didn't believe any of my tricks.

I finally gave in, but I did not like admitting that. While I was feeling defeated, I reluctantly packed my bags and somehow got in the taxi with my family. Got to stop writing now I'm in the cab and sometimes I can get motion sickness from writing or reading in a moving vehicle. I'm not going to lie I felt half anxious and half intrigued for the trip ahead because I never been on a plane abroad before. 9 hours later…

I arrived in England Heathrow airport, and after I waited F O R E V E R, we finally left the airport. We then had to grab another cab all the way to Hampshire! I'm off to get settled in my new home I shall write very soon.

Yours,

Amani.

Dear Diary,

Today was a terrible day, since everybody was laughing and teasing because of the colour of my skin! The next day, I gathered up the courage to tell everyone "I am proud of my black skin, my hair and where I come from. I love my life and the ones who are in it". They all apologised.

Yours,

Amani.

The Crayon Box
Ariana Tyagi

There lived a girl called Bean, who loved colouring more than anything.

So, on her birthday, her great grandpa gave her a shiny box of crayons. She was so excited that she ran to her room immediately to draw a nice picture for her grandpa as a thank you present. After she finished drawing the picture, she thought to use Grandpa's favourite colour, grey, to colour it in. So, she coloured it entirely in grey, and did not like a bit of it. It looked overcast and dismal.

Then she picked white, as it was Great Grandma's favourite colour. Honestly, she could not see a thing in the whiteness, and everything looked blank like the plain white sky.

"What's Dad's favourite colour?" she thought. It is blue indeed. She coloured everything in blue and the whole picture looked muddled up.

Then she wondered what Mummy's favourite colour is. Of course, it's purple. Let's just say it looked dreary and too auberginey.

She then asked her brother Freddie for his favourite colour and he said "orange". Bean coloured every bit of the picture in orange. It looked so burning and exhausting. Whose favourite colour will make this picture look perfect for Grandpa? she wondered.

She then asked her best aunt for help, she said, "It has to be the bright and sunny yellow."

Bean coloured in with yellow and it looked scorching and flashy. She was quite upset by this point and did not want to ask anyone anymore, then she spotted her best sloth toy "Slothie" who looked a bit black. So, she decided to go with black.

"Goodness me!" she said. It looked gloomy like a very old picture.

Bean had enough by then, so she thought to go with her favourite colour which is pink. "What can go wrong with pink?" she thought, as it's the best colour ever. She could not believe her eyes. It looked bleak and too doughnutty.

She looked through her window and the trees looked gorgeous in green. Grandpa likes gardening and nature, so she decided to go with green this time. It was too much, greenness overloaded, and she did not like it. Suddenly, she had a bright idea.

Why don't I use all the colours from my shiny crayon box? That's it, why does anything have to be one colour or another? She coloured in the picture with every colour she could find in the box and believe it or not it turned out to be brilliant. She realised at that moment, that a picture looks gorgeous when all the colours come together.

She ran to Grandpa overjoyed and he said, "The picture looks fantabulous, same as how the world looks perfect when filled with colours. Always remember that no colour is better than one or the other, they all fit nicely in their places. Thank you."

500 Words: Black Lives Matter
Jack Bremner

It was Wednesday 27 May 2020, and Mya, Scott and Travis were all in their houses doing their homework when they heard the news about George Floyd. They did a Zoom call to talk about it.

What happened to George Floyd created an opportunity for Travis to tell Mya and Scott about the times he has been treated differently.

"OMG I never knew things like this happened, I am so shocked," said Mya.

"Yeah it's so sad. Things like this happen all the time to me and my family. My parents get pulled over by the police all the time. Black people are five times more likely to get arrested than a white person," explained Travis.

"I had no idea," Scott replied quietly.

"My parents have taught me that if I am ever involved with the police, I have to show my hands at all times, so they don't think I am reaching for a gun or something," revealed Travis.

Mya and Scott were shocked at hearing what their best friend was saying and had experienced. If they didn't have this conversation about George Floyd, they wouldn't have realised that the reason they don't get treated badly is because they are white.

"Travis, I am so sorry this happens to you. And after what has happened to George Floyd, we need to do something," Mya said seriously.

"Yeah of course, now that we know we can't go on as normal!" exclaimed Scott.

"Let's do it, it's going to take everyone to make a change," Travis explained.

The group decided to make posters and signs and go to a protest. When they got to the protest it started off peaceful, but things soon changed. After the protest Mya, Scott and Travis talked about why they thought the protest turned bad.

"It turned bad because the police were using rubber bullets and tear gas," Mya said angrily.

"People are also just angry and fed up of being treated badly," explained Travis.

"Maybe there are people taking advantage of the Black Lives Matter movement to do bad things also?" Scott suggested.

After the protest the group of friends still feel there is more to be done and decide to make a petition for people to sign and go out into the community to talk about Black Lives Matter. They also (especially Mya and Scott) speak to their friends and family, who also speak to their friends and family and so on.

Mya, Scott and Travis became lifelong activists and created an organisation called "Speak Up Against Racism" to help spread the word and the work that needs to continue being done to make sure that Black Lives Matter isn't forgotten. Their lifelong activism ends up putting a stop to racism, it took days, weeks, months, years but they finally made it to the Supreme Court and their bill to end police brutality was passed. Mya, Scott and Travis go down in history for never giving up doing the right thing and helping others.

Always Be Yourself
Maya Ruby Jakhu

Today is the most important day of Alana's life, the Junior Chef 2020 final!

Alana had her signature dish ready and was set to win. Both her parents came from India and loved cooking delicious Indian dishes. She was four when she started helping her mother and grandmother in the kitchen. When she was old enough, she followed her passion and after watching lots of cookery shows and learning new recipes, she finally made it to this point. Alana put on her chef apron, washed her hands and was ready to cook. For the final signature dish Alana was planning to make a dish from India, so she was going to make her halloumi pakoras, mint and garlic dip with salad to go on the side. Everyone at school told her just to make something simple but she didn't listen to them.

In the middle of making the pakoras, she stopped and looked at everyone else's dishes. They weren't doing a fusion of a Greek cheese in an Indian dish with English sides, they were all doing foods of one country. Alana thought the judges wouldn't understand her mix of foods from different countries.

So, she started a new dish. It was signature cheesecake. Soon, it was time for the judges to taste. She was very nervous and a bit uncomfortable because the dish she was serving wasn't the one she planned on making, but she thought the judges would like it more. The judges tasted and said that it was delicious, but she had a feeling that they liked it but didn't love it and it wasn't the best she could do.

The winner was announced as another girl for unique flavours. Alana was disappointed in herself. She doubted her food from her culture and her lack of confidence in her flavours lost her the Junior Chef 2020 title. She was sad about not winning the competition and was ready to give cooking a break for a long time, but just then her mum walked into her room and asked why she changed her dish. She said it was because she thought the judges wouldn't get her flavours. Her mum told her to be positive.

Alana decided she would start a YouTube blog where all her recipes could be shared with the world. In the first video, she made halloumi pakoras, mint yogurt and salad.

The next day she had a look to see how many likes and subscribes she had, and her video had gone viral! There were lots of positive comments and requests for more videos. Alana felt very happy and confident in her cooking and carried on sharing her recipes to the world that everyone loved. Soon, her cooking was recognised by lots of celebrities and famous cooks. They started contacting her saying how amazing she was. When Alana became sixteen, she got her own cooking show and when she became twenty-one, she got to be a judge on Junior Chef. She learnt to trust her judgment and be herself.

Coming Back
Sebastian Witterick

Greg Turbo was a world class racing hero, but his life and passion for racing changed forever due to racism.

You see, Greg was black. It's not something that you think would matter in motor racing, but he was in the minority amongst the white drivers. He was the best driver on the team but was treated differently. He was given the second-best car, and the constant "jokes" over time all became too much for him. So, he decided to leave the sport that he loved.

Many years went by and he started a new life away from racing, but the passion was always there. He watched it on TV and still had other drivers as friends. When he saw the BLM protests on TV, he thought that he wanted to do something to have his voice heard. And he decided the best way to do this was to fight those bullies, return to racing and fight to be World Champion again.

He then found a team that wanted him as a driver. When meeting the team bosses they didn't mention his skin colour once and he knew this was the team for him. He started practising and it was like he had never been away. He heard about a big competition in Florida for the very best racers and knew this was his chance. He flew to Florida and on the day of the race he arrived at the track and saw all the other drivers doing their practise laps. They were all white and he suddenly thought, has anything changed? But then, he remembered why he was here and all the people that were looking up to him.

As he lined up on the starting grid, he had one thing in his mind – the chequered flag. As the lights went from red, amber, green they were off! The commentators were shouting "Greg Turbo is in third place but is hot on the heels of second place", and suddenly he has found some space on the bend and overtakes. Now in second, he can see the race leader in his sights! He stays in second place for most of the race and he realises he's running out of time. If he's going to make a move for first place, he needs to do it now! He puts the pedal to the metal and goes for it! A sneaky undertake! He hits the grass but manages to keep control and focusses on the track ahead, he pushes and pushes and finally on the last bend he's there! Zooming past the chequered flag in first place! He's done it! His car rolls to a stop and he jumps out, punching the air in celebration. He's lifted high in the sky by his teammates and fans run onto the track to celebrate. He's surrounded by children of all colours asking for his autograph and he then realises that no one is seeing his skin colour anymore.

Best Friends
Tristan Agius

EJ has hair which bounces.

Every strand is tightly curled like little springs and when EJ moves each curl looks like it is jumping, like a little kangaroo. His hair is strong like a lion's mane but soft when you touch it, like a seal. It is the most beautiful hair I have ever seen. My hair is short, straight and red so I think I look like a fox. We like to imagine how funny it would look if our hair was all mixed together.

EJ's skin is black. Even in the sun his skin it is still black. But when he falls over, the blood is red like mine. My skin is white, but in the sun, it quickly turns red like a lobster, my sister says. We wondered what it would look like if our skin was all mixed together.

We have a friend called Indie. Her hair is bouncy too, and soft. But her curls aren't as tight as EJ's and her hair is red like mine! Her skin is brown, and she can run really quickly like a gazelle. In the sun her skin does not go red like mine, her skin gets darker, but she does get freckles like I do.

Zach has blond hair. His hair is wavy like the sea. His eyes are green, and he loves to swim so sometimes we think he might be a merman. He's taller than I am but he is older, so I don't mind.

In September, a new girl came to our school. This is how we met Sofia. Her hair is black, but sometimes it almost looks blue. It is straight and long and when she moves it shines like the sun. Her skin is white it is almost like snow, but she doesn't go red in the sun. Her eyes are brown like EJ's, but mine and Indie's are blue.

How funny we would look if we were all mixed together. We could have one blue eye and one brown eye, half our hair would be curly, but the other half would be wavy and straight. Some of the strands would be black, but some would be red and some would be blonde. Our skin would be brown but with freckles too. I hope it wouldn't go red in the sun. We'd be strong like a lion, fast like a gazelle and clever like a fox. We could bounce like a kangaroo and swim like a seal in the sea. We would be magnificent. These are my best friends.

Connie and The Hair Fairy

Hannah Fajimolu

Connie lived with her mum and dad in a tiny village on the outskirts of London.

Connie's mum had always lived in the village, but her dad had moved there from London when her parents married. Connie's family were white and her dad's family were black. Connie felt conscious of this from a young age, as she felt different from the people around her. Connie's skin was a different colour from the children in her class at school, her surname sounded different too, but above all, Connie hated her hair.

Connie's hair was different from everyone else's she knew. Why couldn't she have long straight blonde hair like her cousins and many friends? Connie would cry and get angry at her mum because her hair was so thick, curly and always knotted. Connie dreaded Sundays, as this was hair wash day! For Connie this would mean that she would have to sit for hours whilst her mum washed, conditioned, and then brushed through the never-ending mass of hair until all the knots and curls were smooth. The conditioners, the moisturisers and oils all smelt amazing but to Connie this was always the worst day of the week, even worse than Maths! When they were out in town ladies were always saying to her "Oh isn't your hair so pretty!" or "Oh let me touch your wonderful hair, it's so curly!"

Connie wondered why people had this strange fascination with her hair, that she so disliked and longed to be different. One day whilst Connie was doing her hair for school and putting her school bows into her hair, a vision of sparkle and glitter dust appeared on her dressing table. Connie stepped back in surprise!

"I am the Hair Fairy and I have been sent here on a mission by the Chief Fairy to let you know that your hair has magical superpowers, that no one else you know will have."

Connie thought this was truly amazing, but who had sent her these powers and what were the powers to be used for? Connie sat down on her chair and listened to what the glittery fairy had to say!

"Chief Fairy has blessed you with this hair to make you strong and wise. Your superpower is that you are not to see yourself as different to any one you might know.

We are all the same, but only special little girls are given all the curls like you. You must look after them and show them off to all those around you."

Then, without saying goodbye or letting Connie ask any further questions, the fairy was gone! A few traces of glitter remained on Connie's dressing table. Connie rubbed her eyes. "Was that just a dream?" she asked herself. It seemed so real and true. Connie sat on her bed and thought about what the fairy had said. Maybe she had been specially blessed, and maybe she wasn't so different after all?

The Caves Beyond the Mountains, Bringing Communities Together

Lola Jordan

Deep beyond the mountains, centuries ago, were two caves.

In these caves lived a secret army of soldiers. Each cave was ruled by its own leader and both were strict and as hard as stone. They would not allow their caves to mix. The soldiers had to eat, train and sleep separately. The black soldiers lived in one cave and in the other cave lived the white soldiers. The leaders slept in their own rooms, away from the caves. Separating the two caves was a vast wall, covered in thick, damp moss. No one was allowed to approach the wall – they all had to live as separate communities.

But there was a small crack on the left corner of the wall that the leaders did not know about. But one soldier from each cave did. One of them was Emily. She was a young white girl and was very lonely as she didn't have any friends in her cave. She was also very curious and wanted to know who was on the other side of the wall.

One night, as everyone slept, Emily was still awake. She couldn't stop thinking about the crack in the wall. She silently crept over to it and stopped.

"Hello?" she whispered. She was so stunned when she heard a reply she nearly fell over.

"Hello," said a kind calm voice from the other side of the wall. "I'm Pete, what is your name?"

"Emily," she said.

They talked for a few more hours and for the first time Emily didn't feel lonely. From then on, every single night when everyone was asleep, Emily and Pete met by the crack in the wall and grew very close. They became best friends and they didn't want to be apart anymore.

"Why should we be separated just because we have different skin?" Emily said.

So, they made a plan. They would convince all the soldiers from each of their caves that they must knock the wall down. They would tell them that they would be stronger together and that although they had different colour skin they were all the same, each with their own unique differences.

One week later, at midnight, when the leaders were asleep in their own rooms, Emily and Pete lined up with their soldiers, all armed with hammers and axes, either side of the wall. They were ready to break it down, but they had to be quick. Half an hour later the wall was completely gone and all that was left was a mammoth pile of rubble and dust rising in front of their eyes. As the dust settled, Emily and Pete saw each other for the first time. As everyone greeted each other, they stood hand in hand smiling. Both caves gathered together and walked out as one. Facing them with astonished looks were the two leaders. Emily and Pete cried out, "We aren't many, we are one," and they walked past the leaders as if they weren't even there.

We Can Make a Difference
Billy Finch

It was the deciding game for Liverpool, and they were winning 1–0.

Mané had put them ahead. I love Mane. I love him because he scores amazing goals and he's a great team player. There were five minutes left and I just knew we would win. It was very late for me – I think it was about 9.15pm.

The next morning, I woke up feeling great because Mane just squeezed in another goal. As I came downstairs, I heard Piers Morgan talking about Mane, so I rushed hoping it was good news. I watched the TV and then I heard him say that people were calling Mane names like "monkey" and "potato". Why would people do that? I was burning with anger because I knew it wasn't nice to call people names especially because of the colour of their skin. There must be something I can do to help. I knew what I had to do to help Mane.

The next day was hot and humid. I was still worried sick about the whole Mane thing. Suddenly I remembered my idea – it just had to work. When I got there my cap nearly blew off it was so windy. My tummy felt like it had butterflies fluttering about inside. I glanced up at the East stand of the one and only Anfield. An hour later I was still holding my "Black lives matter" sign. I felt useless and stupid.

Suddenly, a boy said, "Are you protesting?" and I said yes, hoping for something wonderful to happen. Then I looked back and he was gone.

Sighing, I bent down to do up my shoelace. When I stood up, I realised he was there right beside me. Then out of nowhere loads of people came with beautifully written signs and all wearing shining, bright red Liverpool shirts. As we left people followed, we walked round the streets with colourful signs. I felt like I was a warm marshmallow getting roasted on a hot fire, the feeling of a crowd behind you as well as saving Mane and his team, it was lovely. When I got home, I felt spectacular. Then my phone beeped. I quickly read the text and my heart was pounding loudly. I felt like I was the future.

A week later, I was in Spain getting ready for the Champions League final. Jurgen Klopp wanted me to be Liverpool's team mascot and even better, I got to meet the fantastic Mane in real life. As I walked onto the pitch the crowd cheered. Feeling incredible, I knew I had made a difference. We had all made a difference. And guess what? We won the final. The cup was so shiny and glittery with a red ribbon saying Liverpool.

Black Lives Matter
Firdaus Akande

I can't breathe. I can't breathe. I can't breathe.

All blacks should be treated equally. We're all the same and sometimes different and that's what makes us unique. A long time ago, white people came to Africa and promised our father they would give us a good education. They lied to our parents. Instead they used the black people as slaves and changed their cultures and names to white man names. They take the black slaves away, so they don't know themselves, their culture, their real name and where they come from.

So, we need justice. We need respect. We need our culture. We need to be treated properly. We should fight back for justice. All should be equal and should be treated the way how you want to be treated. We're all the same because we all come from our mothers and fathers and God had created all the humans and the world and we all have the same blood, eyes, hair, legs, arms and heart, so we should all remain in peace in the world.

I can't breathe. I can't breathe. I can't breathe.

It's so important that every citizen is treated equally. You're all family and a citizen. We are the same so we should all be in peace. And we need justice for George Floyd because police in the United States killed innocent George Floyd just because he is black. We're all the same. Justice should be all over and we should all live in a peaceful world side by side. Black Lives Matter stop killing us. Every bit is hurting around my neck, stomach, legs and my arms. Being black is not a crime.

Stand up for racism. Where is the love? Black Lives Matter and silence kills. The UK is not innocent. Black Lives Matter. Black Lives need justice. Black Lives Matter. Help us stay alive and stop the bad people from killing us. Black Lives Matter. It's best if we could get racism done and to do the best we can to make the world a happy place, despite the whites who used blacks as servants. And it is so horrible
to make people all about themselves. The coloured people will strike with Black Lives Matter.

Black Lives Matter. Black Lives Matter. Justice for George Floyd. Justice for George Floyd. Justice for George Floyd. Get racism done. We're all unique. We have the

Stop killing innocent people. Stop killing innocent people Stop killing innocent people. Please help us, we need your help. We need justice. No more separating, we're all the same. We should not be judged by our culture and religion and by our skin. Being different is unique and brilliant. I can't breathe. I can't breathe. Justice for George Floyd and Black Lives Matter.

Space Jam 2
Nicholas Weber

Once in Chicago there were two boys named Brian and Tim.

Tim has a wheelchair and Brian has a black skin. Every morning Brian would push Tim to school. They both went to high school, were the same age and loved spaghetti. They did not have any friends apart from each other. They liked to do things together.

But one day, when they were enjoying their lunch, some bullies started to throw food at them and started laughing. The boys were really upset but did not tell anybody. That night, Brian and Tim decided to have a sleep over at Tim's house and watch Space Jam with Michael Jordan and Bugs Bunny. That night, Brian had a dream about writing a letter to Michael Jordan to ask for help as Bugs did.

Next morning, Brian told Tim his dream, so they went downstairs to write a letter to Michael Jordan with the hope that he was going to help them like he did in the movie. The boys sent the letter out, but they didn't get any response for weeks. Time flew and the older boys bullied Brian and Tim for different reasons. They were laughing at Brian because of his skin colour and Tim because he was disabled.

One day on a lunch break where the boys sat down, the bullies took their lunch again. Then Michael Jordan walked into the dining hall. Everybody gasped and couldn't believe what they saw. Even the bullies were shocked.

Michael went straight to Brian's table and said, "Hello my friends. I have received your letter and thought I will come and see you as I was in your area."

Tim and Brian looked at each other and couldn't believe that Michael was there. They all sat down with the bullies and Michael started talking about his childhood. He was in the same position as Tim and Brian when he was 8 because of his skin colour. But this never stopped him becoming one of the best basketball players in the world. The older boys realised that they had made a mistake and promised they would never do it again. They apologised to their younger colleagues and became their best friends.

After school, everybody played a basketball match with Michael. Tim and Brian improved their self-confidence and helped other children who were in the same position.

They had a club called "No more bullying". This story shows that everybody can be a hero, regardless of their skin colour. Michael Jordan is my hero.

Fight for the World
Alexandra Eve Mathie-Russell

It was at this moment I felt calm in the jungle, lying there with Snow and Patch just thinking if there was no hassle in the world, that without fur colour wouldn't life be so much better?

Would animals actually be nicer to one another?

I looked up at Snow and said, "If we all looked the same would it be better?"

"Well," said Snow wisely, "if we were all the same, life would be very dull."

Patch continued, "We are who we are, and nobody can change that. Be proud of who you are, there is nobody more you than you."

We all looked up at the stormy clouds looming.

Snow said, "Come inside sweetie," so we all padded into her cosy cave and I lay down next to Snow and Patch. We snuggled up together, happy in our unity; me, white as snow, Patch, a beautiful patchwork of blacks, browns and greys and Snow, a beautiful midnight black. As we lay there,

I started wondering why an earth Snow had the name she did. I asked her in my sleepy slumber. Her response was shocking to me. Her parents had made the decision to name her Snow to help protect her. They believed by giving her a white name, animals might respect her a little more and that it might open up better opportunities. This made me very sad, here we all were snuggled up together all happy, all equal, yet all wonderfully different. None of this made any sense to me and I fell into a troubled sleep.

I dreamt that night about a world where we all had to be white, or else you were banished from the land. I hated it. My beautiful friends were now forced to leave, I had to stand by and watch them go.

I woke up, my heart pounding so fast. I felt like I was in a hole that never ended! Finally, Snow woke up and asked me what was wrong. I told her all about my dream and how horrible it was, that my dear friends could not stay with me just because of the colour of their fur. Snow saw I had tears in my eyes, and she wiped them off with one of her big black paws. Patch woke up too and gave me a big cuddle. We all sat cuddled up together.

Snow said, "Look we all know that there is no difference having black fur, white fur and brown fur, we can have a peaceful life where no one needs to be made to believe that they are not good enough for this world."

We chatted more about this crazy world in which we live, the one that is so bothered about what is on the outside rather than what is one the inside. Right there and then, the three friends made a pact that together they would change the world.

The end.

Black Lives Matter
Harry Norfolk

Teacher: "Good morning class and welcome to today's history lesson."

Class: *groans*

Teacher: "Today we are going back in time to the year 2020 when as you may remember from last week's lesson, that was when the first Coronavirus had taken grip of planet Earth."

Akuchi: "Was that around the time that George Floyd was killed by those, what were they called… was it the pol-ee-sh?"

Henri: "POLICE!" *Annoyed*

Teacher: "Thank you, children. 2020 yes, over 1000 years ago was also when the murder of George Floyd triggered the global rise of the Black Lives Matter agenda and led to the eventual eradication of white supremacy inflicted on Black communities and the combating of acts of violence and inequalities against Black people. It also led to the creation of space for Black immigration and more support and celebration of Black innovation and helped to eventually eradicate the need for the police and prisons. But does anyone know how it happened?"

Mark: "Was it, that famous football player, Rashford, Marcus Rashford?"

Teacher: "Well, he helped in a way, yes by persuading the government to make sure that all pupils that needed it got free school lunches over the school holidays. He continued to fight racism, ensuring a percentage of places at top schools for Black children and went on to become Prime Minister of the United Kingdom and Secretary General of the UN. His policies paid for Summer School for children that needed it, passed laws to get rid of tuition fees at university for all, he created sports scholarships for Black children in all sports and made sure that all children learned about Black history in schools. He also made sure that all houses built from 2040 had to have a garden or outdoor space. But it wasn't all about one particular person."

Nico: "I remember my Great Great Great Great Great Great Great Great Great Grandmother went on a Black Lives Matter socially distanced protest march to 10 Downing Street. We made a photograph of her and her friends wearing masks into a hologram in our space pod."

Teacher:"Exactly, the anti-racism movement could not have been successful without lots of people like her and like us getting involved to bring about change. Does anyone know how?"

Jamal:"People donated money to causes promoted by Black Lives Matters that needed funding?"

Chantelle:"People signed petitions?"

Ayush:"People voted for parties that campaigned against racism and remember social media, people with influence showed solidarity with the aims of BLM!"

Teacher:"Wow! I am very impressed. You all know so much. Mr Rashford's changes to the curriculum clearly had a lasting impact. Yes, change happened because people got clued up on the racist struggles faced by Black people and also learned more about black history, black scientists, inventors and explorers."

The bells ring

Teacher:"LUNCH TIME! Everyone get out your lunch and remember to get on your space suits if you are going out onto the moon's surface."

Your Hair is Too Big!
Ambar Alvarez Prasad

Ruby was nervous about her first day at secondary school as she fastened her tie and put on her blazer.

She brushed out her amazing curly hair and gave herself a smile in the mirror before walking to school. As she was walking down the corridor, a teacher with her hair down to her hips stopped Ruby.

"Your hair is unacceptable. Tie it up!" she said.

Ruby just stood there, not sure if the teacher was talking to her.

"You appear to be ignoring me, go home and sort out that hair of yours, it's a hazard!"

Ruby could not stop staring at the teacher's hair, dangling freely around her. Afraid of getting a worse telling-off, she turned and headed home to tie up her hair. For Ruby, this took up to an hour and meant that her hair line was pulled tightly back away from her face.

The next day Ruby went to school, confident that her tied-up hair would now be "acceptable".

In her first lesson, students sitting behind her started complaining, saying, "Miss, we can't see over Ruby's hair!"

The teacher turned to Ruby and told her to move to the back of the class. This happened again and again in every lesson.

After a few weeks, the teacher with the hip-length hair asked her, "Ruby, is this still going on? I have already told you once, I shouldn't have to tell you again, your hair is unacceptable!"

Ruby stood face to face with the teacher and heard herself saying, "My name is Ruby Williams and I am proud of my big hair!"

Trembling, she walked out of the school and never returned. She moved to a school where she was never told her hair in its natural state was unacceptable. Ruby has taught us that no child with Afro hair should be treated like this. All hair is acceptable, and none is too big.

Black Lives Matter
Ahaan Tanna

I saw it three days ago.

A remote-control car in the shop window. It was shiny and green, with purple stripes. Green is her favourite colour. I think she will like it. I go into the shop and the shopkeeper stares suspiciously at my smooth skin. I pick up the car and look at it closely. I move towards the shopkeeper to pay for it. It costs $9.59 and I just about have enough. I reach slowly into my pocket and bring out my crumpled $10 note.

The shopkeeper says, "I'm not sure this is real."

"It's gone through the washing machine, that's why it's crumpled up!" I reply.

"I'm calling the police."

I panic. I run. I try to run. I've done nothing wrong. Sirens roaring as loud as a lion. Lights blazing as bright as a ruby. Three policemen rush out of their cars like three cheetahs running for their prey. Handcuffs on. I feel like a criminal. My wrists hurt. The handcuffs are really tight.

Forced into the police car like a pack of wolves pushing
a small animal into their lair. My wrists are hurting me,
and I don't want to get into the police car. I've done
nothing wrong. I kick one of the policemen in the shin.
My heel crashes into his bone. He holds my neck like a
boa constrictor tightening around a tree. I can't breathe.

He throws me on the ground. My face touches the
concrete. The policeman gets on top of me. I can't breathe.
I can smell his breath. It smells of rotten eggs. He puts his
knee on my neck. I can't breathe. I can taste the car fumes
in the air. I can't breathe. I can see people crowding around
me. They shout, "Stop, he didn't do anything wrong!"

I feel my heart beating very fast. I feel my lungs failing.
I can't breathe. Everything goes black. I reach out for my
family. I can smell my mummy's pasta with tomato sauce.
I can taste fizzy lemonade with ice and mint. I can see my
house and my daughter waving from the window. I can
hear the birds tweeting. I'm lifted into the ambulance and
I think to myself why am I here? I still have my handcuffs
on. The paramedics ask the policeman to undo them. The
policeman refuses. He says I'm a criminal. But I am just a
man buying a toy for my daughter.

New Beginnings
Sana Khan

PART I.

Woke up, grabbed a bite to eat. Time for school.

"Hurry up, don't be late It's your first day you fool!"

A new day, a fresh start. My favourite subject is art. Seeing the playground so empty. New faces staring at me.

"Hey you! I'm talking to you," he said. "You don't belong here, blacks are rubbish, whites rule!"

2020. The school is empty. Sitting in the locker room, scared and frightened. Bang, crash, boom. Someone hears me. The teacher stomps in with an angry face, pointing to the other boy. I've lost this case.

The next day I was anxious, yesterday I was sad. Disappearing from it all, running away, not going to school, forever.

PART II.

Waiting in the corridor, eying up my next victim. Where's that new black boy, the one I saw yesterday, the one I beat to the floor?" I wonder. Little did I know, the black boy was another no show. Minutes, hours, days passed. No way that this would last. I didn't want this to happen. Didn't realise my words would cause so much action. Am I to blame? Could we all live in harmony? Are we all the same? I spotted him from far away. Is it him? I think it is, Should I stay?

PART III.

Head down, tears on my face. I feel so alone. Why am I being beaten up? Is it because of my race? In the distance, I could see that boy who hurt me. At school, a few weeks ago. He's walking down the street, I'm staring at my feet.

"I truly apologise," said the boy.

I had mixed feelings in my mind. Could this be a sign? That he's changed? From that time on, we became best friends. Doesn't matter what will happen, we stand by each other, forever.

Stop Racism
Quinn Loubser

My black friend Tuoyo was being considered for our football team but then the coaching staff changed their minds. I think it had something to do with the fact that Tuoyo was black.

I asked the head coach why he wasn't going to be on the team, as he is such a great player with lots of skills. Tuoyo can run as fast as lighting.

The coach said, "He is always late for practices and we don't think he will be able to afford the kit.".

The coach sounds like he is being very racist and unfair towards Tuoyo. Coach is a dragon and it's going to take the rest of the team to put a stop to this. I spent days talking and trying to convince the rest of the team to help me but they were all worried they would lose their spots on the team. But I finally managed to persuade them to stand up for Tuoyo with me.

Tuoyo said to me, "I am not sad but rather infuriated, even if I'm black, doesn't mean I'm a bad person or player."

The next day me and the team went to our coach and made the following statement:

"If Tuoyo can't play then neither will we."

As we said that, you could see the look on Coach's face.

Coach bowed his head and said, "Fine, Tuoyo can play."

We cheered, lifted Tuoyo in the air and chanted TUOYO TUOYO TUOYO TOUYO. Soon after this incident, we won our first trophy at a school competition and it was all thanks to Tuoyo and his last-minute penalty.

After that great game Coach decided to make Tuoyo captain of our team, which was our first ever black teammate and captain. In fact, he was the first and only black captain in the Richmond borough.

Still to this day, Tuoyo and I are best friends in secondary school, still playing football together. There are also many more fantastic players on the team, who are there because of how they play and not the colour of their skin. My story reminds us that racism is like dirt, it's everywhere and it's often difficult to get rid of. It takes a team effort to clean it up.

Ahmed's Show-and-Tell
Billy Trapp

It was a crisp, Friday morning and I was at school. It was
show-and-tell day.

My friend Ahmed's turn to do his show-and-tell
came around.

"My show-and-tell isn't really a show, it's more of
a tell", he said. "I'm supporting the Black Lives Matter
movement. You might have heard of it. I think it's important
that black lives should be treated exactly the same as
everyone else because we're equal. There's a march at the
weekend, and I'd like as many people as possible to join
me in taking part."

Everyone's hand shot up, apart from mine.

"Yeah let's do it" and "sounds great!" everyone said
excitedly.

But I was the only person not saying anything.

"What about you Will?" Ahmed asked me.

"I'm really sorry, Ahmed, I've got the triathlon regional
championships at the weekend."

Ahmed looked crestfallen, but I think he understood.

Later that night, in bed, I thought about it. I was torn between this amazing cause my friend was so passionate about, and my lifetime dream.

The next morning, looking on teams, I saw, one by one, everyone who had been so excited for Ahmed and who agreed to going, dropping out. Timothy said he was seeing his gran. Oscar said he was playing with Jasper. "I need to walk the dog", "I'm sorry I've got to do homework", the list went on. Soon enough there was no one without an excuse. It was wrong. It was sad. It was heart-breaking. Our friend was so passionate about this cause, and suddenly his picture of him and all of his friends supporting it together, was crushed. I told my mum what had happened, and she said it was my decision what I wanted to do.

The morning came around, and I still hadn't decided. But after my bacon sandwich, I knew exactly what I wanted to do, and knew what was right. I wanted to go to the march. Telling her my decision and that I was sorry, rather than saying she forgave me, she told me how proud she was of me.

We drove to the city centre, and I saw out of the window, a huge gathering of people. The crowd felt threatening, and I was scared. But I thought to myself, "come on Will, it's right and you know it's what you need to do". I saw Ahmed in the distance, in his favourite clothes – an orange bobble hat and Liverpool football top. I jumped out the car and ran as fast as my legs could carry me over to him, giving him the biggest hug ever. His face lit up and he was surprised to see me. We stood together, shouting and holding up signs that read "BLACK LIVES MATTER". We began walking with the rest of the crowd. That moment I knew I had done the right thing. I was proud to stand with my friend and show our broken and torn world what was right.

The Wind of Change
Eden Winning

I looked down on the Earth below; crammed with injustice but also with hope.

I have watched the world from when you were all the same and lived in one place – Africa. I blew the seeds from the trees you used as shelter and I cooled you down when the day was hot and dry. I was there when the slave trade burst into being, destroying not only the lives but the hopes of those enslaved. I was there when the fight for equality began. I was there. I remember.

I remember rushing down chimneys and seeing thin, worn bodies. I remember seeing farmers give away their produce for little money. How unfair this world had become. I remember watching Harriet Tubman steal away into the night to rescue slaves, Rosa Parks saying "No!" when she was told to move and Maya Angelou talking for the first time in 5 years. I am here. I floated purposefully around the world, watching the passionate protesters waving their signs and shouting for equality. I join in the march, pushing their banners and flying their flags. I am here.

I continue my journey, hearing different languages chanting the same things: "Black Lives Matter" and "We want equality". I blew harder at those sitting at home watching the marchers and urging them on silently in their heads but not doing anything to help. I encouraged those fighting and channelled my anger to those trying to silence the fighters. I am here to turn over the pages of history and I implore you to make a change. The future of the world is in your hands. If you speak, you make a difference. One word can change the world forever. One action can change the world forever. Do this and a big change will come. It is your turn to come forwards.

Black Lives Matter!

Diary Entries Based on Ruby Bridges
Rachel Lawrence

Dear Diary,

I went to a white school for the first time today!

However, it was not what I had pictured; some men came in a car to take me to school. When we got there, the men told me not to look back at the shouting crowd. I was very frightened. People shouted horrible things at me and called me rude names. When we finally got in, I had to sit in an office for the whole day! I think I even fell asleep at one point. None of the teachers liked black people so they refused to teach me that day. I had to bring in my own lunch to school because even the cooks refused to provide me food. At the end of the day, the huge crowd was still there but the kind men were here to protect me. Then they drove us home for dinner. I was very hungry.

Dear Diary,

Today a new teacher joined the school! She was white but actually wanted to teach me. I ended up in a class by myself with no other kids. My teacher was very nice. Every lunchtime she would leave the classroom and eat with the other teachers, and I was left alone. The men came and picked me up from school. Once again, I had to go through the crowd. I scurried into the fancy car and we drove home. When I told all my family about my second experience, my dad suddenly looked very worried and asked if I was okay with having a big crowd shouting at me. I explained how scared I was but told him that I got used to it. Actually, inside I hated everything in my school apart from my teacher.

That night I could not sleep at all, so I decided to clamber into my parents' bed and share my emotions with Mum (who was awake too), she told me not to worry and put me back to bed. I lay worrying.

Dear Diary,

Today was a lot better than the previous days.

They put me into a class with other kids! I loved the company. Many of the kids do not play with me but one of the boys asked if I would play football with him. I had never played football with a white person, but I agreed since I had never played with any other kids at my school before.

He seemed nice. I asked if he wanted to be friends and he said he had always wanted a black friend. I was very happy to hear that. He agreed to be friends and said that even if people did not like other people with black skin, he would just ignore them. I told him the right thing is to stand up for yourself and help all you can. The boy played with me every day and we played the best of games. I knew that I would probably have a lot more friends soon.

The Golden Statue
Edward Willis

Once there was a very selfish giant.

This giant had too much gold that he kept for himself. The giant had power over everyone. Even though he was selfish, some people liked the giant and were amazed whenever he spoke – even though it was nonsense. This giant was mean about people who were different, especially people who had different coloured skin to him. To show how dominant he was, the selfish giant decided that he would have a statue built of himself. He wanted the statue to be made of pure gold. He thought the statue would prove that he was the best person in the world. He decided that the money of the land should be used to pay for it.

His advisers said, "That is such a wonderful idea, oh great giant." But inside they thought it was a terrible idea because many people in the land were poor, especially those who had different coloured skin.

The selfish giant ordered the statue to be built, it would take many months and need many people to build it. His advisers told him that they could not afford to pay for people to make the statue because they had paid for the gold.

"Who cares about that?" said the selfish giant. "There are many black people out there who we'll make build the statue for nothing."

So, the selfish giant sent all the black people to work to build the statue. Hour after hour they worked on making the huge golden statue. The people got very little sleep, they became ill, they began to starve.

Then one of them said, "I have a plan." He told the others, they carried on working on the statue, but every night a chipping and tapping sound could be heard.

After many months, the statue was ready. The last sounds of chipping and tapping were heard far away. The selfish giant was glad that the statue was complete – he couldn't wait for it to be unveiled with a parade and a huge party and ceremony. The selfish giant insisted that the black people watch the unveiling as he wanted to show them that he was the best.

The day of the unveiling had arrived. It had been decided that the selfish giant was to stand by the statue and unveil it. The excited crowd stood staring at the statue cloaked in a huge sheet. The selfish giant stepped forward. He was just about to pull the cord, then suddenly both himself and his statue plunged into the ground. The crowd were shocked. The black people cheered and ran to the huge hole. Their plan had worked. After months of chipping underground they had managed to rid the country of the selfish giant and his reign of terror.

From that day on, everyone lived in peace and harmony, and the man behind the plan became the new ruler. He made sure that everyone was treated equally and that the colour of your skin no longer mattered.

One Love
Ellis Williams

The car door slammed shut as Marley got out of his mum's black, shiny car.

He and Elijah were on a mission to get to the Black Lives Matter protest. The boys were excited as they could hear people chanting loudly: "Black Lives Matter!"

As they walked up the hill, they saw lots of people of all ages, colours and genders. But each person was the same because they all carried a banner to support Black Lives Matter. Elijah looked at Marley with his deep brown eyes. The expression on his face was as serious as a lion's stare. Nothing was going to stop them today. Suddenly, from out of the bushes, two boys appeared causing Marley and Elijah to stop dead. One of the boys was dressed all in black apart from a white cap and white and gold trainers. The other boy, who was taller, wore a white tracksuit. Marley and Elijah noticed that the boys also held a large banner above their heads. As they got closer, Elijah tapped Marley nervously. He could see what was written on the banner. Unlike everyone else on their way to the protest, the message was different. It said, "White Lives Matter". The boys approached Marley and Elijah aggressively.

The taller boy said, angrily "Why is it all about black lives? What about white lives? Don't we all matter?"

Marley stepped forward. He was shaking inside but tried hard not to show it. "Listen guys. We are all in this together. It is not against white people to say that black lives matter. It is because all lives matter and we are all the same race – the human race. The colour of a person's skin should not matter but when black people are being treated badly around the world, this is not okay and we need to show up to let everyone know that this must not go on."

Elijah said, "Of course all lives matter but this is a protest for black lives because we have not been treated the same as white lives."

Marley continued: "We are not asking for special treatment. All we are asking is to be treated the same. Is that so much to ask? Black people have had harder times. White people have good times. They never have to worry about being treated differently because of the colour of their skin. This is what we are talking about."

Marley's nerves had disappeared by now.

He went on. "Our differences are what make us special. No one is better than the other. As they say in Jamaica – out of many, one people."

The two boys were silent. Marley and Elijah could see that the boys were thinking carefully about what they had told them and were remorseful. Marley and Elijah were jubilant – they had made a change! They carried on to the protest as proud and happy as could be. They went down on one knee, put their fist in the air and shouted "one love".

Pamela's Journey
Thalia Stevie Hart

One sunny summer's day Pamela set off to visit her beautiful granddaughter who lived in Devon.

Pamela loved an adventure, she loved to travel but most of all she loved to visit her granddaughter. Pamela moved to London from Alabama when she was nineteen, to work for Her Majesty the Queen. She kept the palace tidy. She polished the expensive picture frames, scrubbed the huge hallway floors and she watered the Queen's plants. Over time, Pamela became very good friends with the Queen, and she was treated fairly.

Unfortunately, Pamela became retired due to old age and stopped working for the Queen. She missed listening to all the Queen's adventures. Pamela eventually arrived at Victoria bus station. She steadily walked over to buy her travel tickets. Her heavy bag brushed against her tired legs but she looked forward to the journey ahead. At eleven o'clock, a small red bus pulled into the station. Pamela hurried to the doors, climbed onboard and handed the ticket to the inspector. The bus seemed packed with loads of people and there was only enough standing room for her. Pamela was never one to make a fuss. She placed her bag in the bag holder and held on tight as the bus pulled out of the station onto the main road. Most of the journey she was able to hold her balance, but she found some difficulty going around roundabouts. On one sharp bend, her old tired legs wobbled, and she toppled left onto a young suited city-worker, who was most annoyed as she crumpled his newspaper. She toppled again to the right onto a young lady who was texting on her mobile. Pamela apologised quickly and was most embarrassed. Pamela tried to hold herself steady.

Finally, the bus journey came to an end. Pamela felt very tired and exhausted but was still very excited to see her beautiful granddaughter. Pamela had to wait for yet another bus to take her from Plymouth to the small village where her granddaughter lived. She had fifteen minutes until the next bus arrived, so she walked tiredly into the park and sat on a bench next to a bronze statue labelled – Rosa Parks. Pamela sighed with relief. She was glad to finally sit down, although only for a short moment. Suddenly, a mysterious, kind voice spoke.

"You look like you need to sit down and take the weight off your feet."

"I certainly do!" sighed Pamela. Pamela couldn't believe she was sat talking to a statue. She obviously needed a rest.

Time quickly passed and the bus soon arrived. It was packed full of young schoolchildren on their way home.

As Pamela walked tiredly down bus aisle, a small young girl spoke. "Would you like to sit here?"

"How thoughtful of you dear," replied Pamela. Pamela sat down to take the weight off her feet.

"What's your name?" asked Pamela.

"Rosa. My name is Rosa – after a special lady who stood up for what she believed!"

148

A Wonderful Childhood
Niamh McCandless

Kate is 8 years old.

Her cousin Alison is six months older. They both have a younger sister; Jane and Grace. Whilst Kate only has one sibling, her cousins also have a baby brother George. They do not live close to each other, they're about two and a half hours apart. Kate loves to visit her cousins, so the grown-ups and the children can catch up. Her cousins have a lovely big garden; their uncle Edward loves his flowers and cutting the lawn on his ride-on mower. They love playing together and having sleepovers; they stay up a bit late having fun! Kate and Alison love to play on the swings and chat about all sorts. They also play with George whilst Jane and Grace play and clean things – they love cleaning things! Some years they spend Christmas together. They also like to go on holiday together. They love holidays in Scotland, where they play outside for hours and go on walks that their granny leads (she really likes walks and knows the hotel grounds where they stay, like the back of her hand). Their dogs Sally, Jess, Jura and Poppy love the walks as much as they do! They like to play a game called "Kubb" which their auntie Tanya and uncle John bought for them – they explain the rules! They love to go swimming – twice most days! Their granny and grandpa don't like to go in the water, so they watch their grandchildren from the side. They always dress up for dinner in the evenings – they love the food, it is delicious! They have lots in common and really enjoy getting together as a family.

So now reader, I want to ask you what you think these families are like? In your head what colour skin do you think they have? Was your first thought that they were white, or did you even consider their skin colour? Well, Kate and Jane are white, and their cousins and auntie are black, but their uncle is white like them. Until Black Lives Matter started, Kate never thought about her cousins' skin colour. Kate loves her cousins and sees them just like her. She is sad to think that some people judge others by their skin colour and treat them differently because of it. She thinks all people should be judged and treated the same as white people because people with different skin colours are not alien – they are human just like her. There is no excuse to treat people differently because of their skin colour as it really shouldn't matter to anyone. Kate is white and nobody that she knows judges her on her skin colour so it should be the same for black people too. Kate's parents tell her that people should only be judged on their actions and she thinks they are right.

From Wakanda to the White House
Hanaa Chaudhry

Melanie was a black girl born in Wakanda who moved to America at a young age. She had a dream!

A dream that to most would seem impossible. She wanted to become something very big! She wanted to become the president of the United States! When Melanie went to school and told everyone what she wanted to be she got laughed at.

"Are you crazy? You're black," said Olivia.

"And you're a girl!" laughed Bob.

Melanie held her tears in all day but as soon as she got into the car, her tears streamed down her face like a waterfall.

"What happened?" Mum said in a sympathetic voice.

Melanie looked up and whimpered, "I'm black and a girl. I am never going to become president!"

Mum looked her straight in the eyes and said "Anything is possible. No matter if you are black or a girl." Melanie felt stronger and repeated quietly, "Anything is possible."

The next day, Melanie had a maths test and she had

practised hard. She ate her breakfast while looking at her textbook then headed straight to school. The maths test was now. Melanie was feeling really positive as she knew it was her time to shine! She had her pencil in her hand and started. She got full marks! Melanie was determined and worked hard. She won lots of competitions and prizes, yet no one thought that a black girl like her could get the top job. Why should the colour of anyone's skin stop them from achieving their dreams? The answer was it shouldn't!

Ten years later, Melanie was at university and was studying science with her teacher Mr Rooney, who knew all about Melanie wanting to be president. Unfortunately, he was not very supportive. She was very close to getting a job.

Another ten years had passed, and time was going fast. Melanie had a job working for the President! The President was very old, and he wasn't racist. He actually liked Melanie and he wanted her to be in an election!

Melanie said excitedly, "I would love to… I mean, sorry Sir, I would love to!"

When the day of the election arrived, Melanie had practised her speech fifty times and she had only one question. How could a black woman like her win the election? When Melanie was heading to the election, she texted her mum that same question. Her mum didn't answer. Soon it was time for the election and Melanie still thought she wouldn't win because she was black. She stepped on the stage anyway and saw that more than half of the audience were black!

When she looked down at her phone and she saw a message from her mum saying, "I gathered as many as I could." Melanie was overjoyed and finally began to believe. It was a miracle. She had won!

A few days later, there was a celebratory parade and everyone, black and white, were chanting the words "Black lives matter!"

Amazing Friends
Emily Rose Ball

One day, there were five little girls. Sophie, Lily, Anna, Iris and Eliza.

They were all in the same elite gymnastics team. They were all amazing at all aspects of the gymnastics, including dazzling moves with gigantic flips, with incredible hand stands and magnificent cartwheel displays. The girls were National Champions and were aiming for Olympic success. But one day whilst training, the girls noticed that there was something wrong with Eliza and that she was not her normal self.

"What is wrong Eliza?" asked the girls.

Eliza said, "nothing" and she turned away shyly into a corner, looking noticeably upset and unhappy.

The girls wanted to do something about it, but they did not know what. The instructor also noticed that something was wrong with Eliza and she needed to find out what the problem was to try and resolve the issue. So, when the girls were warming up the instructor pulled

Eliza out and had an extremely long chat about what had been happening lately with Eliza.

"Eliza, what is wrong?" asked the instructor.

"I feel like I am the odd one out because my skin is black and my hair is different to the other girls, they all look the same and I just feel like a lost soul," replied Eliza, sadly.

Immediately, the instructor knew she had to do something to help Eliza.

The instructor decided to stop physical training on that day and instead she focused on Eliza. She asked the girls to describe one another to the group. To Eliza's amazement the girls described her as a wonderful friend with bright eyes, a heart-warming smile and an infectious giggle. Some girls said that she was the best gymnast in the group, with the best, funky moves. In fact, one of the girls was jealous of Eliza's beautiful hair. The girls at this training session all felt very happy, elated that they had helped their friend and gymnast team member. Eliza left the session with a massive smile on her face and skipped happily out of the door.

The next day the girls made a brilliant gymnastic dance routine, with Eliza as the lead.

When Eliza came in the girls taught her the whole

dance and said, "We did this for you. You're not the odd one out, everybody is different."

And they all performed the dance beautifully. All the girls realised that they are all important as individuals, they did not have to look exactly the same as each other, and this is what makes them unique and special.

Laura's Chapter
Darcy Pakes

There were three babies waiting to be born, but they were not quite finished.

Melanie the Melanin Fairy was new to the job and was worried she'd get it wrong. At eleven years old, she finally got the job of her dreams: to add colour to the babies' skin. Carefully, she sprinkled a little bit of Melanin powder on baby Alfie and gave him lots of freckles across his nose and cheeks. With baby Charlotte she was more confident and sprinkled a lot of Melanin powder on her.

"Oops," said Melanie, because there were large blotches everywhere. She sprinkled some more Melanin powder on to fill in the gaps and was very pleased with the golden tanned skin of baby number two. Melanie still had lots of Melanin left so she gave the third baby, Laura, a really good sprinkling and made her skin a nice dark shiny brown. The Melanin Fairy was so pleased with her work making the three babies so different, that she decided to make lots more of each colour.

Melanie watched the babies as they grew up and found that Laura was always being picked on because being white with freckles or tanned is more popular. One day, Melanie found Laura in jail and asked Alfie & Charlotte why. They told her that they went shopping for new books and had spent hours in the bookshop. They piled all kinds of books into their baskets and once there was no more room, the teenagers went to the till.

The lady at the till smiled happily and asked, "Why have you spent so long in my shop?"

"It's our favourite shop because we LOVE reading, just like Matilda!" said Laura, making a heart shape with her hands.

The friends paid, took their receipts and ran out of the shop smiling with excitement. There were two police officers outside, looking around as they always do. Nobody noticed as Laura's receipt fell out of her bag and silently floated away in the wind. The police officers were suspicious of the teenagers because they were running out of the shop. They thought they might have stolen something.

"Let me see your receipt," said the male officer angrily to Laura. Nervously, Laura's cheeks went pink as they looked in her bag. The receipt was nowhere to be found. Charlotte and Alfie stared at the police officers as they explained to Laura that she was going to jail. Melanie, Charlotte and Alfie decided they had to help because it wasn't fair. They had all bought books and were all running from the shop but only Laura was taken to jail. They asked lots of people to make posters and take them to the police station.

Everyone held their posters up and shouted, "We should treat black and brown people the same as white people because they're just the same under their skin!"

Inside the jail Laura heard and was happy. Melanie was proud of her babies.

The New Headmaster
Ayaan Alam

In 2100, Garfield Secondary School looked like an ordinary school.

All the children were doing their regular schoolwork but after the half term, the children were given precise portions of "water". The "water" was a mix of rare chemicals and a microscopic chip. Then after 24 hours, the head robot came into every class and took the children to the planetarium. The head robot only brings the children to the planetarium if it is an important announcement. He rolled in front of the desk and simply shut down. Slyly an UWH (unidentified walking human) casually strolled in.

In a thunderous booming voice, she declared, "Hello children of Garfield School. I am your new headmaster as there is a malfunction in all of your teachers." She said teachers like it was a word she had never spoken of. "Anyway, I will be sorting you into houses, blacks and whites," she pursued. "If you have black skin you go to the black house and if you have white skin you go to the white house," she stated.

She also said her name was Mrs Vlei. There was one child who didn't move though, and his name was Ahmed. Ahmed had black jeans and a puzzled face.

"I command you to move," Mrs Vlei boomed.

All the children started walking around except Roy, Lizzy and Ahmed. Mrs Vlei gave them a hypnotic stare and softly uttered, "Very well, children have a drink of water from the water fountain."

"Why not from our bottles?" Roy, Lizzy and Ahmed simultaneously spoke.

"Because… um… well because it is the cleanest water in the town," panicky Mrs Vlei stuttered.

The children knew something was off about this new "Headteacher". Why were all the children listening to Mrs Vlei's every command? They had to find out. The children rushed to the water fountain and took a sample of the water and took it to the science lab. In their normal school, they were learning how to separate liquids to find how they were made so that was a relief because they knew what to do. Ahmed was the smartest so he started by pouring the water into the beaker and put water from his bottle into another beaker and added citric acid to both of them. The water from the water fountain had an unusual effect while the normal water created carbon dioxide. Now they knew something fishy was going on and it was up to them to find out what. They had ruled out confronting Mrs Vlei because she would make them forcefully drink the water. Then Roy had an ingenious idea. If they could work out how to reverse the effect to make the children out of headmaster's spell. Ahmed somehow achieved to convert the outcome, so then Lizzy sneaked back in the planetarium and supplied the children the water and barged Mrs Vlei into the lake. Then they turned "on" all of the educators. Mrs Vlei's real name was Mrs Evil!

Children Make A Difference
Sophia Morrison

Maya, a little girl, remembers going to the play centre with her mother.

A rainbow of friends playing without a care in the world. Wet and soggy dummies, bottles and beakers were exchanged or popped into each other's mouths. They touched and felt each other's faces and hairs. They were faces of fellow human babies. Each with its own unique beauty and texture. She remembers being on the buses seated in her pushchair surrounded on both sides by friends in pushchairs. How they chattered, curious about each other's pram toys and oh how they laughed at their own babbling. There was no colour.

Yes, she remembers seeing a little boy just like her on the bus not so long ago. No colour noticed they just looked the same age. She smiled and asked him his name, and she told him hers. Like larks learning to pray, they talked about their nursery schools, how big and strong their daddies were, what their favourite colours and foods were.

They talked and talked! The people on the bus could not help but say "Wow, look at that! How beautiful! Children are so innocent! This is how people should relate!"

Then came the gloomy six o'clock news. Watching the breaking news each time sent Maya's heart pounding heavily against her chest. The local Recorder, The Evening Standard all had something to say... someone had been racially abused. Somewhere in London a person had been attacked and the police have said it was racially motivated! There was also news of shootings of black people by the police in America. One day, Maya heard on the news that George Floyd in America had been killed by the police. This time it was not by shooting but the deliberate kneeling on his neck. Sadly, Maya's heart sunk. Why! Why! How could a fellow human being, a policeman for that matter, do such a cruel thing? Maya remembered her beautiful happy memories. Suddenly her heart dropped like an anchor!

She muttered to herself. "I thought we were human beings created equal. I thought children made a difference in the world. I thought as innocent children we had showed adults how to live in harmony." Oh, how wrong her memories were! She wished for this racism to be over. Seeing all the people protesting made Maya even sadder because she felt as a black person she didn't have to protest for her rights over and over again and worst still scared because people could get shot at for protesting.

At the same time, she felt the protests were a way to show and express how she and others feel to a much wider audience. She felt a bit of hope as she knew Black Lives Matter and it shall be well one day. She believes children will make that difference now and in the future. Black Lives Matter. All lives matter. One day all forms of racism will come to an end for good.

10-13
YEARS

⬅ PRAISE FOR THE WINNERS

WINNER: Kristofer was Quiet in School Today
Lucy Moxey

Of the winning story the judges said:
"I loved how you portrayed the perspective of someone in a privileged position so well."
— *Malorie Blackman*

"There's so much control in this piece, it's remarkable. It deals with the issues of BLM so poignantly."
— *Frank Cottrell-Boyce*

"There's an outstanding use of the refrain and it truly is a top, top story within a poem."
— *Francesca Simon*

"It's a very powerful and moving poem, I learnt so much about different people's point of view from it."
— *Charlie Higson*

FINALIST: Computer Says No
Eleanor Hancock

What the judges said:
"I liked this story a lot. The focus on one specific person and their impact is very powerful."
— *Malorie Blackman*

"It's a very specific, accomplished piece that's well structured and rhetorically powerful."
— *Frank Cottrell-Boyce*

"The use of dialogue to portray the characters is very clever and the title is really memorable."
— *Francesca Simon*

"The first line draws you in immediately. It's a controlled piece that knows how it wants you to feel from the start."
— *Charlie Higson*

PRAISE FOR THE WINNERS

FINALIST: Bapa
Samuel Martin

What the judges said:
"What a well told story! The last line is particularly poetic."
— Malorie Blackman

"This was a very unexpected story, it's a lovely piece that felt very real."
— Frank Cottrell-Boyce

"You told an important and historic story with such confidence and warmth."
— Francesca Simon

"I loved this story! It's written so fluently."
— Charlie Higson

FINALIST: Martin Luther King had a Dream
Lani Haria

What the judges said:
"I love the urgency here, the last sentence is incredibly poignant."
– *Malorie Blackman*

"This is a very enjoyable read and it brilliantly brings to life a very powerful message."
– *Frank Cottrell-Boyce*

"This is such an imaginative response, the mixture of historical facts with storytelling is brilliant."
– *Francesca Simon*

"What an excellent idea to write about and brilliantly executed."
– *Charlie Higson*

WINNER:
Kristofer was Quiet in School Today
Lucy Moxey

Kristofer was quiet in school today. When I asked him why, he told me he was late home because him and his mom were stopped by the security guard in the grocery store. I remember when that guy helped me when my bike had a flat tyre. So, he obviously had a good reason to do what he did. He's a good man. After lunch we did science. I hate science. It's so hard. But Kristofer loves it. I have no idea why, but he's very good at it. He is very smart.

Kristofer was quiet in school today. When I asked him why, he told me his mom still hadn't found a job. I remember months ago Kris said his mom was looking for a job. I don't know why, but I expected she would have found one by now! My mom found a job in only a few weeks! He was quite sad about it, so we played his favourite game at recess. He'd bought his toy gun into school (he's not allowed, but I didn't tell). That game seemed to cheer him up a bit. We had so much fun, but for some reason my mom wouldn't let him come over after school.

Kristofer was quiet in school today. When I asked him why, he said he and his older brother had "the talk" I don't know what that means... so I asked him. He said that boys with brown skin had to be told what to do when a cop approached them. Why though? Police are there to protect us, doesn't he understand that? Police are our friends. Kris told me he heard his parents say that "there were guns in our area" whatever that means. Then we played soccer. It was super fun. I like soccer. Kristofer was quiet in school today. When I asked him why, he said he was watching the news and his dad told him to go out the room. But he peeked at it anyway. He saw riots, and police and signs that said "BLM".

What's "BLM"? Why was Kris watching the news anyway? It's boring. I never watch the news. And why would Kris's Dad tell him to go out the room? There's nothing to hide, like I said, it's boring anyways.

At lunchtime we played tag. I was it. But when I went home my mom told me I couldn't hang out with Kris anymore. I was super sad about it. What did Kris ever do wrong?

Kristofer was not in school today. He might have caught the bug, I thought. It's spreading. The teachers called us in to assembly. Our teacher was crying. She told us Kris is not coming to school today, that he's never coming to school ever again, whatever that means. She said the police had thought the toy gun he had was real. I don't understand. I'm scared. I wish Kris were here so I could ask him what this is all about.

RUNNER UP:
Computer Says No
Eleanor Hancock

It's only 9.17am but already one of the saddest days of my life. I lost a friend today.

I met Clayton Palmer about 4 months ago. I'd just started volunteering at the shop at Hammersmith Hospital. He was sixty-seven years old but looked older, with big hair and kind eyes that smiled when he told me about his old life – "the before". He was proud of his Caribbean heritage, and loved to talk about famous Barbadians, although he claimed all the West Indian cricketers, no matter which island they called home.

We got chatting one grey afternoon, when he came in for respite from the rain. In his dripping coat he settled in front of the shop. I offered him a warm drink. He asked for a tea with two sugars – his voice was London with a soft Caribbean lilt. The TV was on in the foyer showing sobbing people leaving cards and flowers near the ruined Grenfell Tower where the horrific fire had happened a few weeks earlier.

"It's a cryin' shame," Clayton said. "Life is cheap in this city when you're poor and brown."

I must have looked taken aback as he immediately said, "I'm sorry Miss, I'm just so angry about that fire. Almost eighty people died in that tower, eighty souls. For what? For the sake of a few thousand pounds for cladding."

I didn't know what to say, so I gave a muffled "sorry".

"I know I look a bit rough to you Miss, but I wasn't always homeless. In the before, I lived in Notting Hill in a council flat with Mum – almost all my life. Mum brought me over from Barbados on the HMS Empire Windrush in 1959, when I was 6. I was scare-cited when the boat docked in Tilbury but I had never seen so much grey!"

He paused. "Mum was a nurse in this hospital for nearly thirty years, with the sick children. She's passed on now – and that's how I come to be here. I told the council she'd passed away and that I would be responsible for the rent. They called me into their office and told me flat – I didn't exist. "COMPUTER SAYS NO!" he said loudly. "See, I came over on my mum's passport and never got one of my own; I never saw the need…" His voice cracked. "Welp, I don't have that choice now. I'm a non-person here and it's in the lap of the Gods when I go now…"

He was being deported to Barbados. I said nothing – what can you say when a person's life is destroyed in an instant? I last saw him a week ago. I brought him a pack-up from home this morning but he won't be coming. He sent a message through a street friend to tell me he'd gone back to the sun. I'm screaming inside. Clayton, was, no, is, a real person.

His life matters. It matters to me.

RUNNER UP:
Bapa
Samuel Martin

My little sister Bea reckons I should change the title of my story to "Grandad". She thinks people won`t understand who my story is about. Mum doesn't know but at school I do refer to him as grandad – it's just easier that way.

My name is Sam. I was named after my Bapa who was also called Sam. Well, his name is actually Mubarak, but when he came to England at seventeen years old, he was told he had to change it to Sam or Jo. Bapa chose Sam.

Stepping off the plane from Nairobi and beginning his life as a dental student at Guy's Hospital must have been a huge adventure for Bapa. The furthest I have been from my hometown in Hampshire is to Staffordshire to visit Grandma and Grandad. It was still an adventure and the temperature difference was probably comparable as grandad doesn't believe in central heating!

The stories of Bapa's student days are brilliant. He had a close-knit group of friends and they caused havoc in the phantom head room (apparently this is a room of robotic heads to practice drilling teeth, not as spooky as the name suggests! Bapa dissolves into hysterics and his eyes glint with mirth when he recalls sending an old lady to the canteen for a hot cuppa having just fitted her new dentures – only to discover later that he had in fact fitted her with wax build-ups rather than the acrylic end results!

He is less animated when he retells his first attempts to get a job post qualification…

Ring, ring, ring.

"Hello?"

"Hi! My name is Sam. I'm a new dental graduate from Guys. I believe you have a vacancy for a dental surgeon?" Bapa has been to an international school and has a cut-glass English accent.

"Why yes sir, we do, would you be interested? We could see you this afternoon for an interview? What did you say your name was again?"

"It's Sam. Sam Samji."

"Oh … I'm… I'm terribly sorry my mistake the vacancy is gone."

Minutes later Bapa's friend Di Davis would phone for the same job and get the interview. Weirdly the position was available again.

Bapa met my Nanny-Ma and they got married. The neighbours blanched to witness a divorced white woman buying a house but they were in danger of spontaneous combustion when moving day revealed that the divorced white woman came with an Indian husband!

Nanny-Ma had a hard time in a mixed-race marriage but she gave back as good as she got. Once a neighbour asked, "What colour are your children?"

Without missing a beat she answered, "Oh, they are blue with pink spots!"

Bapa owned his own practice in Dorking and despite a bumpy start became a well respected (loved even – if you can ever love a dentist!) member of the community. His biggest mental anguish these days is – who should he support in the cricket? He will always be my Bapa not Grandad.

RUNNER UP:
Martin Luther King had a Dream
Lani Haria

Martin Luther King once said: I have a dream that my four little children will one day live in a nation where they will not be judged by the colour of their skin, but by the content of their character.

I have a dream today. I was there in the throng of the crowd as he spoke. The sound of freedom — it was exhilarating! The very same evening, I met with Martin. I didn't know how to tell him about my project. Instead, I said, "If I tell you, you won't believe me. Let me show you, it will all make sense."

He was intrigued and followed me to the basement of my home. Dust mites swirled as I pulled down the curtain and showed him my creation, my time machine. I asked if he wanted to go to the future to see if his dream would come true. My heart was thumping in my chest louder than a hammer. Would he believe me or think I'm mad?

He looked at me with star-like eyes and whispered, "Yes, I want to see if my dream can be real." I grabbed his arm and pulled him into the time machine before he could change his mind.

"When shall we go to?" he asked.

"Six generations into the future," I replied.

With a whir and a click the dial read 28.08.2093. It was one hundred and thirty years since his speech. As we stepped out, the White House stood tall and proud in front of us. The President of the United States was giving a speech. We froze in amazement as she introduced herself.

"My name is Violet Luther King. I address you today, just as my great, great, great grandfather did one hundred and thirty years ago on this very day."

Martin fell to the ground weeping – his future granddaughter was the President. Suddenly, a very official looking car stopped in front of us. Violet climbed out of the car and said, "I don't know why but somehow I know I must talk to you."

"I am Martin Luther King," he replied. "This wonderful young woman has bought me to see the future."

Inside the White House, we sat down and explained everything. Violet told us about how much life had changed for black people. I cried listening to how in the 2010s black people were still treated badly; and how the Black

Lives Matter movement came to be. People from all races, colours and religions coming together to fight for equality.

After a long slow battle for equality, things finally changed in 2063 – a century after Martin's speech. I will never forget the pride in Martin's eyes as we sat listening to Violet. His dream had come true.

Martin Luther King made his speech in 1963. It has been fifty-seven years but atrocities against black people still happen. I don't want to wait till 2063 or 2093 for freedom, for acceptance. I want 2020 to be the year when the whole world agrees that Black Lives Matter.

Wizard of Black Lives Matter
George Hover

Dele was the king of wizards. A wizard with a blue hat and a purple cloak and his one goal was for peace in the world. He was the one that all the others went to with their problems, but there was one big problem he couldn't fix or at least he thought so. Others had tried for hundreds of years!

The problem was called racism and it all started many, many years ago and the wizards had been trying to solve it for just as long! The Clan of Wizards just couldn't work out why and how to stop the non-magic people seeing difference with colour of their skin. They tried every potion and magic word they could to bring harmony, but those intent on seeing the insignificant differences in each other fought against it.

Some kind humans did what they could, they protested peacefully and sang but felt ignored. Some things improved, such as the stopping of slavery and apartheid, but not enough – they just couldn't see why they weren't treated as equal just because of their skin, it didn't make sense! They finally thought of something – a spell but not just your ordinary spell it had to be a very powerful spell and combined with the magic potion.

Dele's quest began on his faithful broom and he first went to Brazil to find and gather the laughter and innocence of children in his magic glass jar, free and not tainted with prejudice. *Woosh* went his broom as he flew past a fire-breathing dragon and the wizard quickly obtained the passion and fire coming from the dragon knowing this would be ideal!

Then *zoom* to India for peace and acceptance, an important spice in his recipe! The final destination was Paris where he soaked up as much love as possible using his magic sponge. He squeezed every last drop he could.

"The world could do with a lot of this," he thought. Dele spent weeks squeezing and mixing his potion. It glistened and smelt like the most beautiful perfume.

Enough was created to cover the world and carry out his plan. Wizards chanted "Black Lives Matter!" and the potion started to bubble and was shining like it had the Sun bursting out!

The wizards dashed to all four corners of the Earth

and splashed it freely, Dele himself charged around on his on his broom. The sun was shining brighter; magic dust shot out of his wand, the dust bubbled and frothed as it went through earth's atmosphere and it suddenly shot down like a bolt of lightning.

The dream had come true, the love was for all to see and he had made everyone as equal and they were blind to colour. They could all get the same chances at life. A tear came out of his eye, it was all everyone had ever wanted! Black lives matter and now everyone got it. Let's hope this beautiful, essential magic rains like a monsoon in our world and makes it a better place!

Moonlight Dance Rehearsals
Hilary Esomugha

"Move this way, Daniel," I said. "No not like that, like this, to the right."

I pointed my right hand up diagonally whilst simultaneously bouncing on my right foot to the right, and doing the same thing with my left hand, to show him what I meant. He followed suit, but quickly slipped and fell on his bottom, screaming out loud in pain. The moonlight dance rehearsal was not going well.

The moonlight dance is a cultural and traditional dance, where a group of dancers dance together around a bonfire under the full moon. This dance is usually performed on the eve of the traditional wedding of any Igbo couple. The couple getting married were my uncle and aunt. My uncle had put me in charge of the dance, it was a great honour and I had to get it right.

The setting of our moonlight dance where we rehearsed was outside the grassless front garden of my family compound. We waited earnestly for the full moon to appear before the rehearsals could start. The full moon signifies joy, excitement, happiness and light, hence why the Igbos have chosen the coming out of the moonlight as a significant time for married couples to do their first dance together. It means starting their lives together in joy, excitement, and happiness, it means they would be bathed in light.

"Nneka!" I screamed. "Bring out all the wooden chairs, the moon is out…"

Nneka, let out a whistle-like sound to signal other participants in the dance to come out.

"What arrangement do you want for the chairs?" she retorted.

"A semi-circle," I responded, whilst gathering all the traditional musical instruments to be used for the dance, such as ichaka, iron gong, bamboo drum, long wooden whistle, and short iron gong. During rehearsals there were always people who would want to watch and enjoy us doing our dance practice. They noticed as soon as the moon came out, and before long the arena was full of eager spectators waiting for the rehearsals to start.

"The absolute first thing we must do is run onto the stage energetically," I said with a loud voice. "We have to be organised while running onto the stage." I then proceeded to show them what to do by running energetically and smiling. "This is what we must do when we run onto the platform tomorrow. Everyone stand still now, form a circle and hold your neighbour to the right and to the left, and move in and out in an octopus-like manner."

Finally, we finished our moonlight dance practice and were all so proud of ourselves. Quickly, I ran into my uncle's house and told him that we were ready for the big day tomorrow; I told him we had perfected the dance. He's him, happy to have fulfilled my part in his wedding; I knew the dance was going to be a huge success.

A Little Black Girl
Adaeze Ulebor

A Little Black Girl Who wants to be a doctor,
Who just so happens to be intelligent,
Who grasps that fact she can't because,
Black girls are aggressive and loud,
Simply not doctor material.
A Little Black Girl, Who learns nothing about her History
from school,
Who's Black for more than 1 month of the year,
Not just for Black History month,
Who's sees Black TV personalities,
Only when BLM pops up.
A Little Black Girl, With black curly hair,
With hair that is prodded and played with,
Whose favourite Disney Princess was Tiana,
Since she's the only one that looks like her.
A Little Black Girl,
Whose athletic team faced racial slurs,
Simply because the team was full of black kids.

A Bigger Black Girl,

Who still wants to be a neurosurgeon,

Who still doesn't like her hair being touched,

Who still wants to change the world,

Who still likes sports,

And Who realises, Rosa didn't give up her seat,

Martin didn't express his dream,

Maya didn't write her endless poems,

Just so she can worry about being treated different.

Ambitions
Isabella Badcock

Alesha's eyelashes gently flickered as she was slowly roused from her sleep by the comforting aroma of banana fritters and coconut bread and the melodic sounds of Mama singing and dancing in the kitchen to a Calypso tune playing on the radio.

Alesha could hear her grandma's boisterous laughs, claps and cackles of approval. The frying pan sizzled away, its fragrant smell announcing yet another important event for the Williams family. The last time there had been this frenzy in the kitchen was at Baby Leeroy's christening last Easter when all the Caribbean families from St William Street had excitedly gathered in the living room, all dressed in their Sunday best, enthusiastically drinking Papa's best home-made rum. Alesha had feared their fragile home might tumble to the ground that day.

Alesha stretched out her arms and twiddled her toes as she leant down to rattle her money box, filled with precious coins for her new sparkling leotard. She accidentally pulled Grandma's hand-knitted blanket off Amoya, who was sleeping soundly at the other end of the bunk.

"Ouch, give it back!" yelled Amoya, as the entire bunk bed rocked back and forth. Little Tiyana, momentarily startled by the noise above, moodily put her thumb in her mouth, shrugged and went back to sleep. Mama had been worried Tiyana might fall so Alesha and Amoya were instructed to "top and tail" but they argued incessantly.

Alesha pulled back the curtain. She had worked out that if she squinted hard enough she could just about make out the balcony of her best friend Liana's flat. It was lovingly strewn with a row of knickers and socks, all neatly pegged on the washing line where Liana lived with her nine brothers and sisters.

The familiar sound of the 8.57 London to Victoria whooshed past on the tracks below, past a tiny patch of green grass corseted by graffiti-coloured walls and rows of identical terraced houses. Alesha followed the groups of boys on skateboards and bicycles scurrying around and bashing their footballs against the concrete walls. She thought she saw Lloyd her big brother up to no good again. Keys turned in the front door announcing Papa's return after his long night shift as a security guard.

Poor Papa, he hated working nights but the pay was good and it meant Anthony could get the books and uniform he needed to get into the Sixth Form College in September, if his grades were good enough. Poor Anthony sometimes had to do his homework in the bathroom because it was so noisy.

Alesha had joined the Gymnastics Club and learned triple back somersaults in no time at all, despite the disapproving glances of the other girls as they laughed at her braided hair and second-hand leotard. She tried her best to brush them out… but it really hurt. That, and the comments about the colour of her skin. Papa rushed in and handed Alesha the envelope. It said "International Olympics Committee invitation"…

End Racial Stereotyping

Lucy Thompson

The evening sun cast long shadows on the ground. The streets were less crowded now. The workers at Tim's shop gradually headed home, leaving him to see out the last hour alone. While Tim was stacking a shelf, the door creaked open. He greeted his customer with a cheery "Good evening!"

The wiry old man with blotchy white skin stared at him with an angry frown. A few silent moments passed as the customer browsed the shelf, then suddenly he turned to face Tim with beady, aggressive eyes. Anxiously looking in all directions, he pointed a knife and growled, "OK, I'm about to take some goodies and you shall be ever so kind to let me have them free of charge, alright?" Without hesitation, the old man reached over the counter and grabbed as many cigarettes and bottles as he could carry and sprinted for the door.

Tim ran after him, but the man had vanished without trace. Tim returned to his shop, gasping for breath, trying to find his phone. The door opened. For a second Tim thought it was the thief returning, but instead it was a young black man, wearing a hoodie, who Tim recognised as Jamal from his estate. Jamal noticed the worried look on Tim's face.

"Sir! Are you okay?"

"Sadly not," said Tim. "I have left my phone at home. A man has just stolen from my shop and I need to call the police!"

Jamal listened with concern. "OK, here's my phone," he said, "you call the police and I will go after him."

Jamal ran after the old man who had barged past him moments earlier. He spotted him down an alleyway, putting the stolen items into a bag.

"Hey, thief!" he shouted. A police car was parked a few feet away from the alleyway, and the officers heard the commotion. The thief began to run but was grabbed by Jamal, who snatched the bag off him just before the policemen arrived.

Jamal said with relief to the officers, "Thank goodness you're here, this man is a th—"

"Silence!" the tall policeman shouted, as his colleague forced Jamal's hands behind his back.

"But sir…"

"Hands behind your back! You are being arrested for robbery."

Jamal was being bundled into the police car, watched by the smug old man, when Tim came running over.

"What's going on?" he gasped. "Oh I see what's going on here! This young man is no criminal, he was helping me catch that thief who stole from my shop," he shouted, pointing in an accusatory manner at the old man.

The thief tried to run, but the other officer captured him.

"OK, I shall let this man go," said the policeman, releasing Jamal.

"Oh no, not just yet, you will apologise to him!" demanded Tim. "I shall be calling the police station to report this to your superiors. You accused this man straight away! Because of the colour of his skin? END RACIAL STEREOTYPING! EQUALITY FOR ALL!"

The Terrible Truth Behind the Tale
Kristen Enoch

Goldilocks. One word, many connotations. Thief. Criminal. Brat. The word "innocent" does not come to your mind, does it? Surprisingly, I am. In fact, allow me to tell you my story.

Firstly, picture me in your head. You're probably thinking of a young girl with fair skin and a mane of gold ringlets. Actually, I am the complete opposite. I have a deep mahogany complexion and a halo of black curls surrounding my face. You've probably heard my fairy-tale. It can be summarised as "Goldilocks broke in, destroyed everything and promptly ran away. The Three Bears are good; Goldilocks is bad."

However, how were the Three Bears able to obtain sugar to sweeten their porridge? I was born and raised in Benin, West Africa. I adored my home, my family and my friends. Everything changed the day they came. They had skin as pristine as snow and wore the most extravagant clothes. They spoke in a rich and enchanting language that captivated anyone who heard them speak. A wide assortment of tools was used by these new visitors, ranging from silver swords to ropes.

I approached them cautiously, eager to meet one of the many newcomers. He did not want to be greeted. He pushed me to the floor and pinned my neck using his knee. A choked cry for help forced itself up my throat, and I felt tears gush down my cheek. I was attacked and packed into the bottom deck of a cramped ship. Transported over several thousand miles, I was forced to work in the scorching sun on a sugar plantation.

My Masters would often use some of the sugar I harvested for their own personal use. I had three Masters: a husband, his wife, and their son. I was permanently brandished with their family name on my back. They often told us that we were worthless, insignificant and inferior. Our lives did not matter. We were whipped, beaten, and struck. Every scar holds a painful memory.

As I lay in bed one night, I had a dream: one day people will not be judged by the colour of their skin, but by the content of their character. The following day, I decided to go and venture into the Masters' house when the family was having a walk. I quickly guzzled down all of the scrumptious porridge – I felt the warm, sweet substance run down my throat.

Unfortunately, the three Masters came back early and caught me. I ran as fast as my weakened legs could carry me; I ran until I couldn't breathe. Thankfully, I escaped. I have never looked back since. My Masters decided to tell my story in order to warn others about trespassing onto their property. In their version of events, I was blonde, pale and evil whilst depicting themselves as harmless and loveable cuddly bears. People then told this story to their children for generations, unaware of the dark reality shrouding it. The truth always hides sinister secrets.

Hope
Archie Jackson

Hope. Headphones in. Music on. My feet hit the footpath, each step matching the rhythm of the bass. Head down.

Arriving at the bus stop, I glance upwards, a sea of faces swimming before me. My gaze fixes on the old lady to my left, she's seen me, and holds her purse just a tiny bit tighter to her chest as I approach. She's not the only one, the suited man hastily moves to the other side of the queue. Head down.

Assumption: a thing that is accepted as true or as certain to happen, without proof.

The bus is heaving, but there are a few empty seats dotted around. I make my way towards the back of the bus where I see a space, I don't fancy standing all the way to school. Reaching the space, the young woman already seated, slides her bag and coat across the empty seat. It's a subtle move, but I see it. I see everything. Awareness stirs and rumbles in the pit of my stomach like a creature awakening from years of slumber, hungry and restless. I wait patiently for her to acknowledge me. I stand all the way.

Prejudice: preconceived opinion that is not based on reason or actual experience.

Fist pumps, high fives and elaborate handshakes are the greetings being shared as I walk through the school gates.

Mr Prichard catches me in the hall. "Best be seeing you at training tonight. Can't let your natural talent go to waste."

I nod reluctantly, but my stomach tightens. I don't want to go. The morning passes in a haze – like most mornings. Chaos ensues as the bell rings for break time; girls gossiping; boys playing football; and teachers nursing their mid-morning coffees like new-born babies. I take a moment and reflect; here at school is where stereotypes unfold. We all are part of the problem. I'm hustled to the football pitch by a group of boys.

"Bruv, we need you, you're designed for this sport."

How hard is it for them to understand that football isn't my thing? Why can't people see me. I mean REALLY see me? I feel the creature in the pit of me stir. It's angry.

Stereotype: a widely held but fixed and oversimplified image or idea of a particular type of person or thing.

The afternoon, much like the morning passes in a foggy blur. The slurs, comments and thoughtless remarks feed the monster within. Headphones back in. Music on. Heavy footsteps pound the path. Unsurprisingly, the bus is packed. I brace myself to stand for the journey home. I don't bother looking for a seat. My thoughts are broken by a tap on my shoulder. Instinctively my body tenses, ready to defend myself, but as I turn, I am greeted with a smiling face.

"There's a seat here if you want it?" I feel something new, hope.

Hope: a feeling of expectation and desire for a particular thing to happen.

The Girl in the Dress
Amelie Muir

The girl in the dress. I never saw her face, not even a glimpse. No one did. She was at the front of the protest, in a bright green dress. From the distance, we heard the echo cries of those being pepper-sprayed, shoved to the ground, beaten out the way: by the police. At this instant, she tore the "Police" tape with her bare hands and stepped foot onto the road. She has to be careful, because each step could be her last.

By her side, clutched with either hand was a white board, with black writing, I couldn't make out much of it, until out of nowhere, she raised it above her head with all her might and slowly started chanting along with it.

"No peace! No justice! No peace! No justice!"

After a while, many people from all around started to join in with her.

"NO PEACE! NO JUSTICE! NO PEACE! NO JUSTICE!"

It carried on for a while, until a startling shot was

heard from far off. It was the police. Everyone ran back and hid behind the lines of the tape, as if it were home in a game of IT. But it wasn't, there is no home, wherever you go the police will be able to find you. How can you feel safe, when the ones meant to protect you are shooting innocent people and killing those worthy of life? It's not fair!

Everyone hid behind the tape lines, everyone other than the girl in the green dress. She stood there, head held high, with an air of authority surrounding her. Still, towering over everyone, held high was the sign. As the police approached, she stood still, like this was her land and they were the intruders, she was a lion and they were the deers: she was ready to kill.

The police came closer and closer, until their faces were stained in my head. The one on the right, red haired, face covered in freckles, short and chubby. The middle one, slender face, prominent features, quite tall and had long blond locks plaited and hanging from his head.

The one on the left, brown hair stuck to his head as if the tub of gel had fallen out on it, nearly as tall as the others combined, blue eyes, muscles bulging out of his shirt. They came closer with their shields, pushing through the crowds, and as they came closer to the girl, expecting her to run, they were stunned at her reluctance to move from the spot.

I remember what my dad told me, to remember their badge numbers, because this could be crucial if something ever was to happen. The red-haired one: 121. The blond one: 163. The brown-haired one: 201.

I was 9 when I got the talk, about the colour of my skin. I was too scared to stand up to the police, but the girl in the dress wasn't. She sacrificed her life for us. For me.

What Happened Next
Freya Briers

My heart was pounding when I heard a yell and turned my head in the direction it had come from to see men pushing a statue towards the harbour.

"That's Edward Colston He sold over 85,000 slaves in his life, he was racist."

They were walking past me. Without even thinking I was up there next to them, offering to help push the statue. They accepted and I bent down when… I was on the deck of a ship. I was at the front of the ship when I heard footsteps and and turned my head noticing voluminous clothes, a face that I couldn't place.

Then it clicked, this was Edward Colston and the hundreds of black people in chains behind him; just some of the thousands of slaves he transported. Their chains were dragging, they were walking slowly. A white man was standing behind them with a whip raised above their backs.

"Speed up," he said then whipped them. They immediately sped up but one jumped off the gangplank and was only just pulled back up by the others. I stood there, horrified, when a light appeared, forcing me to close my eyes.

I opened them and I wasn't on a ship. I was sitting in a huge bush on top of a hill looking down onto a village. I could see people marching into it with what looked like walking sticks, but I was horrified to realise these were guns. They were firing everywhere, and some people seemed to be starting fires. Screaming was everywhere, nowhere was safe. People started running out of buildings, some bleeding some sweating fiercely. The people with the guns were the sailors from the boat and the villagers were intended to be the next batch of slaves. The sailors started to clamp chains on their ankles when everyone fell silent. I recognised Edward Colston again and he seemed happy with all the slaves now in front of him when another ball of light forced me to close my eyes and…

I was in a town square with a platform in the centre of it. There was a table with a hammer placed on it which made me realise it was an auction. I breathed a sigh of relief until I saw what was for sale. Slaves were in pens behind the platform looking terrified at their fate and they were brought up. The auctioneer sold them with a slam of his hammer and the crowds in the square seemed to consider it a job well done as they shook hands with each new owner and they came to collect their slaves and when the flash of light came this time I was ready and closed my eyes.

I opened them and I was back in Bristol, pushing the statue towards the harbour.

Invisible
Isaac Son

It was a sunny, dry afternoon in South Africa. I heard my grandfather's voice telling me to come to the truck. I got in the truck, and we left. We started driving to the outskirts of the city. The big houses of rich people with swimming pools, grand gates and electric fences gave way to barren spaces with dried grass and red dust.

We followed faded road markings and crumbling curbs. As we pulled up to the large green metal gate, an ageing security guard ambled over and pulled the gate open for us. We drove past the vast rubbish containers of the dump and stopped in the centre of a clearing. We could see hills of rubbish, with washing lines everywhere, a few mismatched buildings and desolate fields of waste.

My grandfather started pressing the truck's horn over and over, the sound echoing back from the surrounding hills. With the returning echo came men, wrapped in mismatched, tattered clothing salvaged from the giant bins of people's waste. They gathered around us, some sitting, some standing, some talking amongst themselves. Their faces bore the heaviness of hardship and the uncertainty of not knowing where they would sleep and what they would eat today. Beanies covered hair, some black, some greying. Shy smiles showed missing teeth. These people were South Africa's illegal immigrants. They had come from Zimbabwe, Mozambique, and sometimes even further away. Many left tyrannical leaders and poverty, hoping to earn money for their families back home. But jobs were hard to find, and shame or lack of money left them trapped in South Africa. Not citizens, not refugees, they were legally non-existent.

But here they were. My grandfather would begin to pray in his broken and accented English, often with one of the men translating my grandfather's words into Zulu or Swahili. The prayer was not long. Some closed their eyes, some clasped their hands, some continued to talk amongst themselves. When he finished praying, he would open the back of the truck and pull out bags full of food packages. My grandfather and I would hand them out, one by one. Some said "thank you" some said nothing, one or two would talk with my grandfather, and the rest wandered off. It was hard to know whether our visit had made any difference to their day, or their lives.

Every week we came, every week we sounded the horn, and every week they sat with us, prayed and ate. But every week we would leave again. Nelson Mandela had a dream of a rainbow nation, where opportunities would be equal for everyone. The men we met were those who did not know this dream, and who could never realise it. They were, and are, invisible.

My Little Hero
M. Zoraiz Mohmand

It all started one summers afternoon, 3 years ago. I was sitting on my most comfortable rocking chair, gazing out of the window when I saw a movers' truck enter our street and park in front a recently sold house. A family car followed the truck. I saw a little 9-year-old boy along with his older sister and their parents get out of the car. The boy had an infectious smile and I instantly liked him.

Soon afterwards, as they settled in their new home, he presented himself with his mum to greet their new neighbours. I had lost my husband eighteen months ago. I was an old lady who was on the verge of finishing life and had enough of everything to do with living! I was ready for God to call for me, to spend all of eternity in paradise with John my loving husband and reunite with my family and my loved ones once again. His mother introduced him as Teo and he was in Year 5. They had moved from Nigeria as her husband found a job in a local company. He had a cheeky grin, and his large hazel eyes were full of mischief and dreams.

I got out of my chair and he helped me with my walker. I went into the kitchen where he followed me and I gave him some fruit bonbons. Soon afterwards, he started coming on his own. He started calling me Granny Edna. All of a sudden, my life changed and in a blink of an eye, I started to feel happier again. He was a part of my world now. We started doing so many fun things together, going to the local shop, for a stroll in the park, to catch the crisp sun on our faces, feed the ducks, and we'd even watch some of the movies me and my husband bought a few years back. He was a grandson I never had.

One day we were out on our usual stroll, where two boys ganged up against us as they wanted to steal my purse. Teo came to my defence but one of the boys started punching him hard and pushed him aside. As they were turning on me, Teo screamed with all his might just to protect me. In doing so, people started gathering around us and one person called the police so the boys fled from the sight in no time.

The police arrived within minutes of the incident. We had explained what had just happened and with a blink of an eye, the whole situation was resolved; the boys were caught and everyone started cheering for Teo, whom I like to call "My Little Hero".

Planet Take 2.0
Joshua Singer

It's that time of year where we come together to remember the fateful events of police brutality that caused the destruction of the planet they called Earth. These historical events caused mass protests and civil unrest which led to destruction, including 98% of the population. Here, we no longer need police, we now have peacekeepers.

The media is filled with captured moments from those times. Who would have thought the earth was going to end that way? My parents, down in the observation lounge of our pod, were discussing the "End of Hate" anniversary, so I decided to ask them the question that had been bothering me.

"How come there's no fighting or protests anymore?"

My parents ignored me. They turned off the home entertainment system and stopped talking. My mother told me to do my chores and left the room. I wouldn't get answers tonight. They were sending me to stay with grandfather for the evening.

My grandad, in his small sustainable orb, welcomed me in from the harsh, dusty atmosphere. As I moved through decontamination, he poured me a herbal drink. He was still eating his breakfast when I asked him about The Anniversary and why there was no more fighting and protests. He avoided all eye contact with me, watching the leaves swirl around in the precious hot water. I was desperate to know more…

It was evening before grandfather finally met my eye. He sighed and opened a small chest, which had been stored under his sleep pod. He opened it to unveil a torn sheet of paper.

Dear Grandson,

The Earth was destroyed following riots and protests around the world after several people were killed by the police because of the colour of their skin. It sparked a movement called "Black Lives Matter". There was no hope for change so the momentous decision was made to start over again. People had had enough of history repeating itself. Hopefully, in the future, you will live in a world where no one is different.

Love Grandpa Joe.

I was shocked. No wonder everyone was so silent and uncomfortable. The knowledge was a secret legacy of shame. Grandad said I had to go to sleep, so he kissed me goodnight, turned off the light and shut the door.

"Wait, Grandad, there is one more thing I want to ask you."

He looked at me and nodded.

"How come there is no more need for fighting and protests?" I asked again.

Grandad didn't answer me for a while, before saying, "Well, on Take 2.0, when we are born, we're born colour-blind."

"What does colour-blind mean?"

"The Earth used to have more than light and shade. There were differences called colours, which are impossible to describe. People feared differences, so now there are none. Being colour-blind means that you cannot see colours; everyone looks the same and therefore are treated equally."

"Oh!" I hadn't realised I was colour-blind.

The Graveyard
Molly Foster

My feet are cold and blistered, and the ground beneath them is soft, freshly placed. I pass the gravestones one by one: Breonna Taylor, George Floyd, Aletaina Jefferson, Aura Rosser, Stephan Clark, Botham Jean…

They are lined up, stretching out into the horizon, an ocean of people, an ocean that should never have existed. An ocean that we will not allow to grow. I carry a bundle of flowers, a few hundred at least, but nowhere near enough for every grave.

Unlike some, I cannot walk through the graveyard and deny that I am privileged to be standing on the ground, not under it. None of them should be here, they should be at school or at work, or with their friends and families. I have a duty to them to know all of their names. So that their memory can live a full life, even though they never got to.

I crouch down at one of the gravestones, the name at the top reads "Freddie Gray". I place my hand on the stone, and ask it to show me his last memories…

All of a sudden I'm in the back of a police car, tied by my hands and legs, the shackles are tight, they hurt. We drive around a corner, and I am tossed off my seat by the jolt of the car. My back hurts. They didn't give me a seatbelt. We swerve around another corner, and I fall again. I can't feel my legs. Another corner, and I'm thrown against the wall. It's so dark. I'm so cold. Why is it so cold?

Back in the graveyard, on my knees and in tears, I read the sentencing of the officers involved… They got ten years.

I find another grave: "Tamir Rice". This one stands out, it's a lot smaller than the others. I place my hand on the gravestone…

I have a plastic gun in my hand, a toy gun. My sister is in front of me, smiling. I lift up my little toy gun and pretend to shoot it at a bird, perched in a tree. We both laugh. I don't see it happen, I just feel the bullet hit my skin, see the officers as they tackle my sister to the ground… No one comes, everything is so dark. I hear my mother's voice, telling me it will be okay. I know she is lying.

Then the pain goes away… I am back in the graveyard again. I read the sentencing of the officers. One of them was suspended for ten days, the other was fired. I gaze out into the setting sun…

The field is vast and bare. Empty graves lie at the back, dozens, hundreds, thousands. How many will be filled? How many more innocent black men, women, and children need to be killed by the people sworn to protect them, before people start to listen? Black lives matter. That should not be a controversial opinion. It should be a fact.

I Love Me
Jaeda Taiwo

I ran. Ran away from school. Away from Kyra King and her jeering remarks about my "big" lips, "flat" nose and "too dark" skin. Hot tears were pouring down my face. I heard my friends, Raymie and Tina calling my name, but I didn't care. They didn't know how it felt. They weren't like me. For once I questioned why my only friends were white. Did they feel pity for me, or was it a dare from Kyra King? No, Raymie and Tina weren't like that – or were they?

I was so busy thinking about my own thoughts, that I accidentally bumped into a young lady. I apologised, but then, I looked up. She was beautiful, although she had vitiligo. Her smile was ethereal and there was no escaping it. Suddenly, my problems seemed so meagre. This woman had vitiligo, but yet she was smiling in a way to say "stare all you want, but it won't affect me".

Oh, how I wished I could be so proud! Again, I was so deep in my own thoughts that I didn't notice the woman peering at me worriedly and asking me if I was alright.

"My name is Shanice." She saw the way I was looking at her and misunderstood. "Don't worry, I won't bite. Now, why are you so upset?""

"I'm Imani," I whispered. A girl in school started mocking me because of my lips, nose and skin."

Shanice seemed horrified. "This still goes on?" she asked. "Of course, unless we're in 2076 without me knowing. Here, come with me." Shanice offered her hand. I followed her, although Mother may not have approved.

Shanice took me to a cosy, chic apartment. There were ginormous glass windows across one wall. Yellow beanbags were shoved into a corner. I gaped in awe at the kitchen. It looked like the one my favourite chef (Sunny Anderson) used! I staggered back at the sight of the seventy-inch TV. Shanice motioned for me to plop onto a beanbag and she did the same.

"You know what you experienced now," Shanice began. I winced at memories of something that seemed so long ago. "That is racism. And it isn't something you should stay quiet about. Tell your teachers, your parents, your friends, your relatives – anyone who'll listen. Because it'll help. Help you, by getting a weight off your shoulder and help them, because they'll feel grateful that you value them as someone you can talk to."

I hadn't thought about it that way before… Shanice cut through my thoughts.

"Oh, and one more thing: you're beautiful. I bet that Kyra is just jealous. You know some women pay people to get bigger lips and hate their pointy noses. Us black folk are lucky because we get big lips and flat noses for free. Unless, you'd rather have lips as thin as a line and a nose so pointy you could prick yourself."

I giggled at the thought of Kyra being jealous of me. I love me.

Becoming
Henry Agius

"All lives matter!" I hear them chant.

'All lives matter!' the crowd demand.

But our voices shall not be silenced this time, by their sound.

Samuel shivered in his bed. The mornings here were dark with a penetrating cold which held only the promise of worse to come, this late in the year. He could already hear the howling wind – relentlessly driving the icy rain against his window – and he quickly pulled the thick duvet further over his head.

Half awake, half asleep, he remembered when each new morning would bring the feeling of the sun, burning, through his still-closed eyelids. The wall of heat which could stun you with its breath-taking ferocity; the sound of the crickets' interminable chirping and the lingering smell of wet dust after it had rained.

He dragged himself, morosely, out of bed. There was no good in all this remembering, he muttered to himself.

He stood in front of the mirror, just like every other morning, and practised rolling his "r"s. If he could just sound like everyone else, even if he didn't look like them, he was sure things would be different.

When Samuel and his parents had arrived in Scotland two winters ago he had expected the stares which ensued – people who looked like him weren't exactly common in tiny towns on the East Coast. But the accent problem, this, he hadn't anticipated. He'd grown up speaking English – along with two other languages – and knew that he was just as articulate as anyone else his age.

Still, the other children at school would sometimes laugh and pretend not to understand him and the moment he opened his mouth the first thing adults would say was always, "Wow what an unusual accent! Where are you from?"

Samuel wanted so desperately to say, "here, I'm from here too!" Yet he knew that this wasn't the answer they were after. They wanted him to confirm to them that he was other, that he didn't really belong. So, he worked every morning, alone in his room, on sounding just like them. To remove one of the last remaining traces of who he once had been.

By now he dressed just like everyone else at school, rejecting the clothes he had grown up in and which his parents still proudly wore. He refused to eat the food his mother cooked from home – even though his stomach growled in furious protest – just in case the smell of other lingered on him for too long.

To be from here, nothing must remain from there he would whisper to himself, over and over and over again until the sound was almost soothing, like a stream running over worn-smooth rocks. Now Samuel scrubbed his skin until it was raw and closed his mind to any more thoughts of there. He chipped and chipped away at himself until he felt the only thing which remained of the real Samuel was his skeleton. Gleaming and white and just like everyone else's.

Silence Kills
Chloe Nursaw

Screaming, shouting and angry talk envelops the city like a
dark cape. Voices raised as they campaign for their rights,
looks and beliefs. Posters fill the air swinging violently
and police on the edges trying to break through but not
managing because of the vast numbers. "Black Lives Matter"
echoes through London leaping from building to building
and street to street.

This world is out of control. But I perch on the
windowsill peering through the window like an inquisitive
bird. Wanting to go down there and speak out all my
feelings and opinions but I am too scared. I am African.
I am Black. The difference between me and you could be
barely anything, but it can somehow be enough to live my
life at a different level.

My name is Jamal and I am seventeen. One day a few
years ago, war spread even closer to my home in Nigeria.
My mum and my sister and I fled away from the slowly
destroyed place we once called home. We travelled on

boats, the back of trucks, any way we could really to get to a safer country. Many a time people with guns spotted us and shot. It was a traumatic experience.

Then weeks later we arrived in England, finally somewhere safe. We were given a tiny flat in a dirty street and this is still where I'm sitting now 7 years later. The colour of my skin led to bullying and lots of it throughout my time at school. Every day I put up with the sneers, the names and the punches, but in my head I've had enough. Why me? What's the difference? Yes, my skin may be a little different but why should this matter? It is not fair. We need a superhero really to turn this world around.

Throughout the years there have been people who have been heroes who have changed the minds of others but where is the one this world needs now? For years I have sat at my window watching protests marching by, but from today I am going to be part of this. I will work towards being a hero. I am Black and I matter.

Now I am on the platform speaking out to my country. Telling them my story and how Black Lives Matter. My video has been shared and replayed millions of times throughout the world. The shouting and the screaming is part of me. The posters some handmade by me. I am not afraid anymore, silence does kill and everyone matters: black, brown, white, Asian, European, anyone, everyone matters.

Maybe one day I'll get killed for my actions but I am not afraid in saying my part, I'm helping everyone not just me. I hope one day people will remember me, Jamal, I was one of the ones who turned this destroyed world into a place of happiness, rights and equality. But this may not happen if no-one speaks out.

Your voice counts. Speak out. Silence Kills.

Marcus
Jielan Mahary

This story is about a boy called Marcus. He was exactly the same as the average boy of his age, he liked playing football, he liked playing videogames online, and he definitely liked being with his friends. The only irregularity about him was one thing, the smallest difference that nobody would notice if they didn't even see him. His skin colour.

Marcus wasn't originally from this country, as his parents lived in a foreign country before moving to the UK with him at an extremely young age. He was a pretty confident boy in all the aspects you'd imagine a teenage boy would be, but of course, as all stories go, he wasn't originally like this.

When he first moved to the UK, nobody made a big deal about him. He certainly noticed an oddly large amount of stares at him when the teacher at his school first introduced him, but that was about it. He was quite shy at the beginning, but he did make a few friends after a while, they informed him about all the trends, where to go, what to do and such, but he never really felt like he fitted in. He did enjoy doing these fun things with his friends but there was something odd about all of it. He did face quite a bit of discrimination from the other children but he never really took any of the hate comments against him seriously.

But just like any other adolescent schoolboy, he started thinking too much about his own self-image. He and his family were walking, talking sandbags to those who wanted to vent their anger because of things that his family didn't even do. He didn't like it. Any of it. This kept on happening over and over again to the point where he just snapped. He changed from how he was before and, just like how he was treated before, he vented his rage onto others, for no absolute reason.

Just a few months ago, he was a timid child who had no reason to provoke anyone, no matter what the case. One day, he was browsing on his phone and came across something popular on the news and social media, it was a movement called #BlackLivesMatter. He read a lot of posts on forums just purely out of curiosity. Then, that curiosity turned to interest. Not long after, that interest turned to hope. He found salvation in the movement as the stories of others were indifferent to his own. He posted his own story and, to his surprise, many people commented on it, talked to him about his life and even asked him to join the movement.

So, he did. He changed quite drastically yet again, but this time for the good. He discussed it with his friends, family and even the teachers, and he started becoming the confident kid like he was before. Even joining some of the protests with his friends. That was how Marcus ended up like he was.

No Justice, No Peace
Deborah Afolayan

Wake up America

We're suffering, we're in pain

Nobody is listening to our outcry

We can't breathe because we're choked by racism

We're tortured because of the colour of our skin

You're hurting us, scaring us, shooting us, lying to us

We're scared to walk around in groups –

Because what we call "groups" you call "gangs"

Why can't you see that killing us isn't right?

Why won't you give us the justice we deserve?

We're writhing in our graves because your silence deafens us

We are Eric Gardner, Tamir Rice, Akai Gurley, George Floyd

We had to die in order for the world to notice us

If you won't give us justice, we won't give you peace

Stop sleeping, America

Wake up!

Wake up Britain

We're suffering, we're in pain

And yet you stupidly think that this is a game
But you've been hiding for too long, and now it's time to
seek
You say that the UK is racism-free
But we can't pay our bills because you cheat us of our income
We can't get a decent job
Without changing our names to seem "more white"
Our mothers are biting their nails with fear
When they discover we got into a fight with a white person
Our children don't understand why no one in their school
looks like them
You say you're blind but we know you can see
You see what we're facing day by day
We are Olaseni Lewis, Sheku Bayoh, Mikey Powell, Ricky
Bishop
We had to die in order for you to notice us
We won't rest in peace until you give us what we want
For God's sake, Britain —
Wake up!

A Second Chance
George Cruise

Peter opened his eyes. The lights were white and blindingly bright. He could hear a babble of unfamiliar voices intermingled with a symphony of repetitive beeps. The ceiling raced above him as he rattled along the never-ending corridor. He could just make out the top of the mask covering his nose and mouth. His breathing was erratic, like it had been for the last couple of days.

Flashbacks played through his mind. The hot sweat that covered him at bedtime. The tightness in his chest when he woke in the early hours. The panic he heard in his wife's voice when he collapsed on the kitchen floor. The blue flashing lights and now here.

A face suddenly came into view. Peter could see dark skin and hair. A foreign voice spoke gently to Peter. "You're in hospital now Mr Jones. My name is Dr Mohamed and we are trying to make your breathing stable. We think you have the virus."

It would usually be at this point that Peter would

complain about yet another "Darky" or mumble to his wife that he couldn't understand a word, but Peter was too weak to say anything. He nodded and shut his eyes. Peter lived in Luton. He worked the building sites all his life. He always said that Asians and Blacks had invaded his country. He got involved with far-right groups. His tattoos told a story. England was his country and he wanted it back. He wanted to make it white again.

And now Peter lay on a hospital table surrounded by people from all walks of life, people who originated from many different countries around the world but settled in Luton and worked day in, day out to save the lives of their fellow human beings. These same people were statistically more likely to catch and be severely affected by the virus and yet they were dedicated to the cause. They would help anybody, even someone who "hated" them for the colour of their skin.

"We're going to make you sleep now Peter," whispered Dr Mohamed. "We need to put you in a coma to help you breathe and clear the virus from your body."

Peter understood. He was gone. Peter woke up two months later. He was extremely emotional when his wife told him how long he had been sleeping. He was weary and weak but had fought off the virus that ravaged his body. His wife could not believe how much he had changed, not in appearance but in spirit and belief. It was as if he had had a revelation while in the coma. His poisoned views had drained from his body.

"I want to see Dr Mohamed," croaked Peter, his voice parched from lack of water. "I want to say thank you."

The nurse looked sad and paused, wondering whether to reveal the truth. "I'm sorry Peter, the virus infected Dr Mohamed too, not long after you arrived. Despite our best efforts he passed away last month."

Coloured Lens
Rose Speller

We all stared blankly at the buffering TV, as the images of screaming protestors flicked across the screen.

"One man, and all of this had happened," I thought. I didn't have a clue what was going on. It couldn't possibly be that bad. It's only taken one person to set off this explosion of protesting and chaos.

The next day was far from normal at school. I walked into school, happy as Larry, not having a second thought about last night's news. As I opened the school doors, I stared at the cluster of people around the Headmaster's office door. I walked over sheepishly, wanting to see what the fuss was.

Being 5 foot 1 inch, I couldn't exactly see over all the freakishly big sixth formers. As if in a snap of a finger, the crowd parted, and a tall policeman was walking with Sam, an African boy just the year above me. What was happening — Sam was so kind-hearted and would never hurt a fly — what could he have done?

I heard whispers around me as the policeman and Sam left the building:

"I heard he broke into the pension home and stole some old lady's fortune…"

"I heard he mugged a woman down Church street…"

"I heard…"

They just kept coming. More and more reasons as to why he was being led out. Sam had been there for me on the first day of school, when some Year 10 boy was deciding to tease me. I looked outside, to see Sam being tackled and shoved into the back of the police car, as his mother sobbed and bit her nails. I walked out, I needed answers.

"Pardon me?" I tapped Sam's mother's shoulder. "Ms Evergreen, is it?"

"Yes dear?" she responded through heavy breaths and sobs.

"I'm sorry to ask you, but what happened to Sam?"

"Oh, you know how people are…" She trailed off but regained her courage. "Someone was seen trying to mug an old lady last night. Of course it wasn't my dear boy Sam, he was busy revising for his exams. The witness said that the boy had a St Juliet's Upper School hoodie on." She wiped her eyes with her sleeve. "But it could've been any of the boys here! Sam is so sweet and good-natured."

I felt anger steaming inside.

"People will find any reason to blame black people, my dear." She put a hand on my shoulder, squeezing me tight. With that, she walked off. What? How could I have not seen this? It was as if I had some coloured lens on, and that I couldn't see the real world. Three weeks later, I was in the streets with thousands of other people, shouting and screaming. This was for every child who had ever felt out of place because of their ethnicity. The colour of your skin does not depict the size of your heart. Your race does not define you. Together, all these people and I will make a difference. Mark my word.

I See
Sally Sheridan

I watch and I wait. I wait for the people of the world to act. I wait for them to fight back against racism across the world. My words may still inspire people, but I wish I was there with them. I wish I was next to them and fighting with them. They are in this fight together. I see how society has changed. I see that people do not admit or accept their racist ways, and they do not challenge society anymore.

The racism is not as apparent, but it is still there. They may not have to sit separately on buses, or go to different schools, but it is still there. It lingers in the air like a grey fog, waiting to discriminate and dehumanize. I see the subtle comments, the assumptions, the silence when they walk in the room.

I see it all.

After so many years, you would think that they would be past treating people differently because of who they are. You would think that they would see people for who they are on the inside, instead of judging them before they even talk to them. After so many deaths at the hands of those who are meant to protect them, you would think that the people in power would be actively doing something about it. But they aren't. They have left it up to them to fight, and they will not stop until they have won. They will not stop until they have equality.

I see it all.

I see the place their world has become. Some say they live in The Land of the Free. How wrong they could be. They do not live in The Land of the Free. They live in the Land of the Powerful, controlling the oppressed. They live in a world where justice is served to the few, not the many. They live in a world where your identity, the colour of your skin, can be the difference between life and death. I am Martin Luther King Jr, and I am watching. I am Martin Luther King Jr, and I am waiting. I am Martin Luther King Jr, and I see.

Imagine
Parinitaa Sasikaran

As you get pulled over by a police officer, the words your mother always used to tell you flash through your mind: "Do not make eye contact with the officer, don't look outside either. Here, take this book and pretend to read it, alright? Remember, don't say anything."

The cop banging on your window snaps you out of your thoughts and you quickly open your window, facing a very stern cop. You gulp.

Opening your phone, your eyes raise in shock before rapidly unlocking your phone, almost dropping it from how anxious you are. Skimming the e-mail, your face drops as you read: "Unfortunately, we do not think you have the skills for this job. However, we have a spot for you to train this gentleman who we think has great potential…"

You block out the rest for a minute and flop onto your bed, tired of seeing and hearing the same words over and over again. As you walk home, you get grabbed harshly from behind. You hear a cold threatening whisper in your ear. Elbowing the person in the ribs you dash, your adrenaline pumping. You hear the faint shouts of slurs and phrases you'd rather not hear.

Walking in the mall, pictures and posters of what society deems perfect surround you, almost towering over you, invading your mind. You walk by the park, overhearing some people.

"…animals 'ey are, 'em blacks…"

"…'ey shouldn't be in this country…"

A shiver runs down your spine and you walk the other way, the walk turning into a run, you don't look back.

"What language do you speak?"

"Hum? I speak English," you answer, confused.

"No, no, no, like, your real language."

"Yes English is my, real, language." You raise an eyebrow.

"No, like, what do your parents speak?"

You answer with a stone-cold face. "English."

They have a confused expression on their face and you sigh. "I also speak…"

"Ah yes, I've heard of that before!" they say. "You act so white!"

"What?"

"Like you're not loud and aggressive or like, ratchet

like the majority of black people, y'know?"

"You have such a white name!"

"Your name is hard to pronounce, can I call you… instead?"

"Look! I'm almost as dark as you with my tan!"

"I'm darker than a black person!"

"If you don't like it here go ahead and go back to your country."

"I don't want to be friends with a black person."

"I don't date black girls."

"Monkey."

"Black girls are so loud and aggressive all the time and for what? Calm down."

"Dark skin can't even COMPARE to light skin."

"Relax! It's just a joke."

"Stop being so sensitive."

"We can't even make jokes anymore?"

"Jeez! Calm it!"

"What a snowflake."

Now imagine this, but so much more and so much worse. Now imagine that as a reality. A young black woman's reality.

Chess
Theo Ziegler

I'm a black pawn who's sworn to protect his King. I do not
have a home or any money – none of us have much, but
the white pieces own everything and they live in luxury.
I get given food at work; we all get little amounts, though
at least it's food.

The white pawns are treated so much better; they
have food, money and homes. It's a war. They want us
dead, but we want equality. The white pieces come first
in everything it's like colour is a priority. However, I would
change that. I will go to the other side to become a knight,
giving me a chance of being heard. Many of us have tried
but been taken and put into slavery.

I will be different. I will be the one. I have one shot.
I cannot tell anyone because they will tell the Queen...
who will tell the King... who won't let me go for my safety.
But actually, how am I different from the others? That's
been stuck in my mind for years. I'm thought of as the weak
one, the odd one out. Really, they are. Why haven't they

thought of doing what I'm going to attempt? Many riots have started from the protests – that's why I'm going alone.

One day my chance came. There was a riot on the other side of the board. I grabbed my dirty water and sign (Black Chess Pieces Matter). I made my way through the board to the other side. I was spotted by the White King. He let me pass! This has never happened before. A change might come. I got to the end. I felt dizzy.

After minutes of swirling around, I steadied myself. I jumped up on a castle and the whites glared at me.

"Overcoming poverty is not an ask of charity, it is an act of justice. Like slavery, poverty is not natural. It is man-made and it can be overcome and eradicated by the actions of us chess pieces. It can fall on a generation to be great. You can be the generation who is willing to help."

The White King sent a letter to my King asking for peace. Both kings signed and later that night a huge banquet happened with food galore and everyone was invited. And finally… there was peace.

All I Can See
Sophie Schagen

I have been standing here in the centre of Bristol since 1977, preserved in death as a statue. I remember the day I was erected, pulled up from looking down at the grass to see the sights. It was a strange day.

Edward Coulston of 1636 was used to the 17th century but here there were so many people, so many new things. I wasn't sure what I had done or what I was doing. I didn't know what I was in for later.

In 1978 I remember the first thing that stuck with me. People had stood under my gaze for a whole year and I had started to understand the society that I was in. I had heard conversations under the trees opposite me, friends, enemies and lovers. This was the first time I had seen violence. Three young teenagers had beaten up a young black woman and had dragged her over to my statue. They stood there, her limp beaten body in their arms, pointing up at my face.

"This man had the right idea. You lot should be locked up."

What? I remembered some of what I had done and regret seeped into my mind. "No!" I wanted to scream at them. "She is just like you! Let her be!"

But they had already pushed her into the grass and walked off laughing. She dragged herself up off the ground and spat at me with hatred in her eyes. I deserved it.

Now, as an angry crowd tears me off my high and mighty plinth and pushes me into the river, I know I deserve everything I get. The crowd jeer and laugh. They have tied me up and in that moment I remember everything when I was alive. All of those documents signed, making real people into numbers. Oh, what a mistake. I should have known better.

As I crash into the water, I try to scream sorry into the harsh air, but even if they heard me, it wouldn't have changed the past. Even a thousand sorries could have not made up for what I have done. I wonder if this powerlessness is punishment from above. The dirty water trickling down my bronze face is the closest I come to tears.

The Book
Niamh Cullen

As the sun disappeared behind the mountains, I opened the book. The book that changed my life forever. Inhaling the delicious odour of Mother's cherry pie, I spied something in the toy box. The huge book slammed onto the floor, as I read the title. "Triangular Trade" emblazoned in gold leaf on the leather-bound cover. I tried to comprehend what this meant as a silver light shone from the first page.

Within a split second, I was suddenly transported to a hut, littered with dust and ashes. I looked down at my body; at least I was still black. A solemn woman sat next to a small fire, cooking meats. She was wearing a beige cloth slung over her shoulder, barely covering her whole body.

Whipping around, I watched other children through the window as they frolicked and played; suddenly their faces turned frightened and they ran into the nearby woods: Why? Strange white men burst through the door of the house I was in.

"Round 'em up!" they cried.

My eyes widened in shock and fright. Muffled by one of the angry men, the woman cried, "Run Enola!" I stared in confusion. I knew I should have run but I knew my name wasn't Enola.

Someone grabbed my arms from behind me and put an uncomfortable contraption around my neck. He shouted, "Put a goree on 'em mates! I can already tell these are gonna be rebellious!" he said, pointing at scars that had suddenly appeared on my arm.

As I struggled, he pulled on the stick around my neck, nearly strangling me to death, as he attempted to put metal shackles around my wrists and ankles. When he succeeded, he shoved me into a wooden cage. Tearstained faces looked upon me with pity, my face reflecting theirs.

Making a loud noise that made my ears want to bleed, a wooden ship could be seen on the horizon, as one of the sailors started shouting commands at the men below. As if we were cattle, they encircled us and ultimately threw us down below deck. I felt scared, as if I would never see my mother again. Salty tears trickled down my red cheeks and into my mouth.

We were packed into narrow rows, every move monitored by sailors on top deck, leering at us. Magically, a silver light shone brightly in my eyes. My saviour had finally arrived. Closing the book, afraid to read further, mother strolled into the room. She stopped cold as she recognised the old crinkled pages.

"Violet, I didn't mean for you to see that!" I collapsed into her arms as I sobbed.

Why were we discriminated against just because we had black skin? That's why now I understand we can do something to gain equality. That's why I can't stand people who are racist. That's why I protest every day and I will keep on doing this until black people and white people can live harmoniously among each other, growing together.

Why Can't They Just Follow the Laws?
Hemani Stallard

Prashant emptied the last of the pretzels into his bowl. The news was blasting through their house: his father never quite understood the TV on low volume. He could hear scattered words like: "protester" "looter" and "Floyd" drifting through the halls.

He walked to the living room to see his parents watching the TV, with their brows furrowed and sporting concentrated looks. The broadcast showed protesters from around the world; Britain, France, Spain all angrily holding up signs and smashing buildings. It showed policemen and the protesters locked in fights and police cars being abused with various bits of rubbish. His presence went unacknowledged as his parents watched the TV.

His father finally spoke to say: "Yeh log kya kar rehe hain?" What are these people doing?

Prashant sat in silence as his mother clicked her tongue. They continued to watch the TV with disdainful faces. It was like a silent message was passed through the kitchen as if to say: "Why can't they just follow the laws?"

Prashant wanted to ask them something, but after hearing that it seemed like a lost cause. His friends were going out protesting today — he knew subconsciously that his parents would say no. Nonetheless he agreed to meet them half an hour from now. Prashant didn't understand his parents most times. Why did his grades have to be perfect? Why must he only date Indian girls? Why was his sister never allowed out? Why did they have to have daal every night? But he was most confused about this: why aren't we supporting each other? It seemed odd to him that his parents were secretly racist toward black people when they themselves were minorities.

"Beta, where are you going?"

"Out."

"Where?"

"To see my friends, I'm going to take Lia with me."

"She is studying."

"She finished hours ago."

His mother hesitated. "Ok Beta, be safe. Don't go near protests, just stay in your friend's house." His mother kissed him on the cheek as Prashant walked upstairs to get his sister. He knew that she wanted to go too, and his parents had previously said no. He came to her room to see her hunched over her textbooks, scribbling helplessly at a notebook.

"Lia we are going out!" Prashant exclaimed standing in her doorway.

"Go away, I'm busy."

"My friends and I are going to the protest and I thought you wanted to come."

"Mom and Dad will find out and I'll be chained to my desk for life. Besides I'm studying."

"You have been studying for hours now and if they find out they find out," he shrugged. "Your call…"

"…Okay fine." Lia smiled as she grabbed her handbag and mask. "But you better say it was your idea if they find out."

They both ran down the stairs and went out the front door.

"Wait!" Prashant ran back inside and emerged holding two signs, both read: "Black Lives Matter".

The Flowers in the Field
Esme Kittle

My chequered school dress flows in the humid breeze.
My scuffed velcro shoes hit the ground as I skip. My mind is
occupied on the flowers in the field, that beam at me every
day as I walk home. They are my friends. They listen to my
thoughts and whisper their reassurance. I want to be them,
the flowers in the field.

They are all so different, but they are viewed as the
same. All have unique colours, shapes, and sizes. They stand
tall together, holding their sweet smiles for me and keep
their heads held high. They are a family, they are united,
and they are flowers in a field.

I sit down beside them and ask them if they judge.
If they judge each other's long thick stems or short
pink petals. They tell me no. They say that each flower is
beautiful in their own way. Millions of delicate faces that
watch me with such delight. I realise each can be damaged
if you hurt it: if you pick its petals away or tread on one
completely. Its confidence to regrow takes a long time to

develop. But the flowers around it also get impacted by the tread. They are leaning and are so weak; they feel damaged and hurt as well.

I stroke their joyous heads. They are happy together; no one bothers them, no one discriminates a flower from their love. I imagine the people I know; they would walk into this field and would not be affected by the different colours and shapes of flowers. They would say that they're just flowers in a field.

I stand up and walk along the path. I stare at each detail of a flower that makes them different from the rest. There are so many for each one: not just the orange ones, or the pink ones, or the blue. They are all completely different. One is tilted, one is much taller than the rest, one is a mix between orange and yellow, one red is darker than another, one has short petals, one has a petal missing, one is leaning over, one has many leaves on its stem, one barely has a stem, two have grown joined together, one has white marks, one has lots of pollen, one has barely any, one is shrivelled, one has some long petals and some short, two are tangled, one has thorns. But if you look from a distance, they are all exactly the same. All the flowers in the field. Without all the flowers, the field would not be as beautiful.

How the Lions Became the Kings
Grace Wagstaff

Once lived a whole community of beautiful, proud lions.
They lived in a leafy jungle. There were tall, towering trees
that lingered over them intimidatingly, and wonderful,
whooshing waterfalls whose water gushed rapidly down
to the ground. The lions sat in "their jungle" day after day
thinking they were alone, but sometimes wishing there
were others…

One fine, sunny day the playful cubs snuck off to
explore! After miles of running and panting they came
to what seemed like a leaf wall. They looked through
cautiously and their eyes widened as they saw a whole
team of panthers. They all looked at each other and bolted
back to their pride to tell all about what they had seen.

As quick as lightning they had all left to try and take
over the panthers, and their habitat. They swiftly arrived
with confidence and no mercy. The panthers had fear in
their eyes and their legs shook a little as the lions spoke
with booming voices.

After weeks of slavery and misery, one courageous, heroic panther stepped up and tried to put an end to this oppression. He spoke loudly with great confidence that he could change the lions' stubborn minds! But it was no use the lions just smirked and chuckled a little, and the next thing you knew the inspiring panther was thrown aggressively into a jail cell made of stone and ebony wood. He was imprisoned.

Although most of the pride found his courage hilarious, the cubs were drawn in by his motivational speech and they were determined to change their elders' views on different types of animal. They stayed up all night trying to think of a plan, in the end they opted to join the panthers and stick up for their rights. They chose this as they knew that the older lions wouldn't bring them to any harm.

Early the next morning the strong-minded cubs went to lay next to the panthers' young and tell them how they felt. The panthers all agreed and when the elder lions arose to tell them to do horrible, tiring deeds they were shocked as they saw their cubs stood proudly in front of the nervous yet happy panthers. The enraged lions went to take a strike at the panthers but pulled back as they saw their valiant cubs standing up for what they believed in.

This had a massive effect on them, they realised that their cubs were stronger and more mature than them. They looked at each other in despair realising their terrible actions. Immediately they let out the sorrowful inspirational speaker and apologised. They went around helping the injured and fixing everything they had destroyed.

The panthers went off talking suspiciously and the lions began to think that something fishy was going on. But to the lions' relief, when they came back the panthers announced that they thought that the lions should become the kings of the jungle! For changing their actions for the better.

Only Human
Ellie Robson

You can drive your car, but carry all your ID,
You can have an education, but a difference you'll see.
You can hang out with your friends, but not too late,
Don't retaliate against insults, the words are only bait.
Work twice as hard as others, to achieve the same goals,
Don't fight back, or you'll fall deeper into their dark holes.
Always use a bag, no matter how little you buy,
Keep the receipt, though you know you don't lie.
Why are these rules,
Thrown into the pools,
Of the way a black person has to act,
So, they are not attacked?
Why do they have to have fights,
For human rights?
Why don't we start rewriting,
The things they are fighting?
Only Human, is what they are.
Although they'll still have the scar,

From being told they're not good enough,
After someone was rough.
Only Human, is what these people were.
Although their deaths, were just a blur.
Tyree Crawford, Anthony Ashford, Rumain Brisbon, Janet
Wilson, Breonna Taylor, Eric Garner, Ezell Ford, George Floyd.
Why are more than these people dead?
Why were these people a small part of a thread,
That will go on,
Long after we are gone?
Why does it have to continue?
You have it within you,
To stand up for what is right.
But you would rather be lounging in the sunlight.
Why are people treated different,
Just because of a bit of pigment?
Why are they any different than us,
When we are the cause of all this fuss.
Maybe not specifically you,
But taking a stand is long overdue.
Only Human, is all they'll ever be.
As well as when they are free.
Only Human, because they cry the same tears

And shout the same cheers.
Only Human, because they smile the same smiles,
And walk down the same aisles.
Only Human, because they laugh the same laughs,
And walk the same paths.
Why is a law made after someone's death,
Passed, after many more had their last breath?
Black Lives Matter, because they do.
Not because of what they have been through,
But because they mattered in the first place,
And your life shouldn't be different because of your race.
Black Lives Matter.
And don't scatter,
Just because you were proved wrong,
Because you knew we were right all along.
Why are the ones who are supposed to protect us,
Not showing kindness?
Why do they confront
And not support the movement?
If you're not standing, speaking out, signing petitions or
donating money,
Don't think you're funny!
You're just as bad as the racist,

And you're no better than the biased.
Only Human, as they bleed, just like us,
And celebrate the same Christmas.
Only Human, as they just want peace,
And for the racism to cease.
Only Human, as they all have ambitions,
And have daughters and sons.
Only Human, as they just want to learn and grow,
And see their children's happiness glow.
We are Only Human

Mikey's Speech
Amelie Philips

Mikey was a ten-year-old boy who wanted to make the world a better place. He was black, proud, had an afro and always wore his grandpa's oversized jumper. He lived with his mum, his dad and his gran. They all lived quite a normal life, but soon that would all change.

It all started with the death of a black man called George Floyd. He was killed by a white police officer in America. It made people angry because George did nothing wrong and protests started against racism because this sort of murder had happened more than once, and Mikey knew it. When he was five, his grandpa was tragically shot by three white men and since then he had been taught to be careful around police.

"Don't move, don't speak," his mum would say. It rang in his head swirling with worries.

"Why should I have to learn this and my friends don't?" Mikey would think to himself. He wanted to make a difference so he made a plan to ask his mum if he could go to the protest and show his point of view.

He asked his mother but she immediately responded, "It's too dangerous Mikey, remember what happened to your grandpa."

It wasn't fair – it just wasn't. That night Mikey saw on the news that protesters white and black were getting stopped for standing up for what they believe in. He understood now what his mum had meant, but he still wanted to make a difference, so he decided to write a speech. The next morning Mikey's mum came into his room to see signs saying: BLACK LIVES MATTER, WE ALL MATTER!

"What is this, I told you, you're not to go to the protest!" she shouted. Then she noticed a long speech. It had every single word and thought that had been bottled up inside her.

"Who wrote this?"

"I did," Mikey replied, "and I plan to read it today. I want to make a difference."

She took a deep breath, what was she teaching her child? "Then I will help."

Later that day, Mikey walked up to his balcony and breathed in. Mikey was just about to speak when his neighbour passed him a megaphone and said, "You deserve to be heard."

Mikey smiled and began. "My name is Mikey and I'm black. I hate racism and I want it to stop because it feels like a cage of worry you can't escape. My grandpa was killed, George Floyd was killed and many others have suffered from this hate. I'm ten years old and even I know this is wrong we all matter and we need to change but we can only change together so who's with me?"

He waited for a response but there was nothing. He turned away, but then he heard it, cheers and roars showed that he was heard. He could make a difference. He did make a difference!

The end.

Black People Can't Swim
Keeley Meredith

"Black people can't swim" is a comment that will stick in my mind forever! My name is Albie Williams and I'm twelve years old and as you may have guessed, I'm black. My parents are both of Caribbean origin but born and bred in England, which is where I was born too.

I go to Valley Academy and have lots of friends there. If I'm completely honest, I only enjoy going to school to meet up with my friends and play sport of course. Yes, you've guessed it, PE is my favourite subject! Well, it was until Mr Adams, my PE teacher, yelled the most hurtful comment when I put my hand up to join the school swimming team. Why would someone say you cannot do something just because of the colour of your skin? I was furious that day and went home feeling so deflated instead of my usual happy-go-lucky self. My mom could tell I wasn't my normal happy self when I stormed through the door that day.

"What on earth happened at school today?" Mom asked immediately.

"Nothing!" I yelled back.

"Well, it doesn't look like nothing, your face looks like thunder," Mom swiftly replied.

I spent that whole evening and every evening of that week researching: swimming, black swimmers, local swimming clubs and best places to swim. My mind was in a spin, but I wanted to prove my PE teacher wrong. Yes, I was still furious, but I felt better once I had done my research and had contacted a few local swimming clubs. The replies came back quite quick and one swimming club asked to see me that very weekend. I checked with my parents, but still didn't tell them about Mr Adams' comment at school. They were delighted for me to go along and meet the swimming coach. Not only was I super-duper excited to get to the Leisure Centre on Sunday morning; also, slightly nervous in case Mr Adams was right. I ran the whole way there and was beaming from ear to ear when I met the coach.

"What's your best stroke Albie?" asked the coach.

"Front crawl," I quickly answered back.

"Right, let's see what you're like in the water, young man," responded the coach.

"Great, meet you at the poolside," I screeched back in excitement.

It felt so good showing the coach my different strokes in the water and not once did he mention the colour of my skin. I was over the moon.

"You're a great swimmer Albie and I would certainly recommend you join our swimming club," said the coach.

"There is nothing I would love more," I replied. So, that was the day I joined "Manor Swimming Club". I loved it there, the swimming coaches were so dedicated and encouraging and I soon had a whole new bunch of friends too. I now own hundreds of swimming awards and have also started to teach the younger children so I can say confidently, "Black people CAN swim!"

In an Ideal World
Korey Belafonte-Lambert

I am walking through the school corridor, Dave's lyrics blasting through my headphones. "Black is beautiful, black is excellent. Black is pain, black is joy, black is evident." I'm wearing a sick suit, it's as comfortable as a tracksuit but it's a smart suit; teamed with black Air Forces with a red, gold and green trim, because wearing comfortable footwear doesn't stop me from being professional.

I used to think that as a child about wearing school shoes, but now I get to wear trainers every day. I laugh out loud.

I get to the office door. It has my name on it. I am the headteacher of the Robin Walker School of Excellence (Robin Walker is a Black British author and historian). In my office there is photograph of my family at a 2020 Black Lives Matter protest. Today is a busy day; interviews for a new member of staff.

As I am showing Jane Wegeate around the school I ask "what made you choose a career in teaching?" I listen carefully to the answer.

I take the opportunity to share my story. "For me it was because of my school experience. I didn't want another black boy to have to go through what I did. Name calling: rude, defiant, disruptive, deliberately obtuse. Being sent out of class. Repeatedly given a detention. Repeatedly sent to isolation. Repeated negativity and microaggressions and punishments when I questioned what was happening. No adults willing to listen. Always being told my behaviour was the problem."

Miss Wegeate: "Wow."

Me: "Now that I am the head, I make sure things are very different."

During the interview Miss Wegeate is asked to describe a time where she dealt with an issue of race at work. "I heard a white student shout out 'Where are you?' to a black student when the lights were switched off to watch a video. I didn't say anything to the child. He had an additional need. I ignored it. I now know that I should have handled the situation very differently. A better example is when I had to call the parent of a black student. The student had said something to upset a teacher. The parent was upset and explained that her son feels that he treated differently because he is black. I reassured her. I don't see colour. I just see the child.''

Miss Wegeate was not offered the job. There were more examples that showed her racial bias. She needs training and educating. Staff that listen, that don't dismiss a child's experience, that value students and their parents is what I want in my school. I sit back in my black, leather gaming chair.

There's a knock at the door.

''Come in.''

The knocking gets louder and faster.

''Come in.''

I sit up. I am in a room. I look around. I am in my bedroom.

''What? That was so real.'' Like Martin Luther King… I had a dream.

To See Through My Eyes
Amber Cotton

It was a ruthless world out there where everyone was judged. Blues were superior to the browns; browns were superior to the greens. These inhuman daily acts of bias left the brown-eyed feeling distraught. They've always been treated differently for some reason.

It had been going on so long that it got to a point where nobody even knew how it started. They had been split up into 3 different factions: faction 1, the blue eyed and the richest; faction 2, the brown eyed, the middle class; and finally, faction 3, the green eyed, the poor. Children didn't know what it would be like to be friends with someone from a different category. I don't know what it's like to be friends with any.

My name's Abigail, but the blue eyes call us chromos. It's short for Heterochromia which is when both of your eyes are different colours. My right eye is green and my left's brown. We're like the factionless. We rely on the kindness and generosity of the green eyes feeding us their scraps. We can't go out. If the blue eyes found us, we'd be done. Mum says they're threatened by us because we're different, I say it's because we disturb the peace of the faction system. I didn't like it one bit. We had nothing for ourselves, it's all from the green eyes. Faction 2 just tend to stay away from us as if we're contagious.

All my family are chromos. We were just used to it. I felt isolated until I met Isobel. We're the same. Except she has blue and green eyes. As time went on, we managed to recruit more and more of the factionless. It wasn't hard, they were just as fed up as us. Things had been too unfair for too long. Within a matter of weeks, whispers of our planned uprising infiltrated faction 3 and support for our cause grew rapidly. Many were quick to volunteer and only a few were hesitant as they had grown up with this system and were concerned about their future if we joined forces.

Isobel and I along with the new recruits started protesting for equality and rights, to convince more to join us in our crucial mission to stop treating others differently because of something so small and insignificant. After enlisting lots of people like we had hoped, we moved on to our next challenge. Faction 2! It was the most difficult obstacle we'd faced but we were ready to fight for what was right.

As we approached, we realised that they had begun to shield themselves, obviously aware of our arrival. The streets were empty with nobody to listen to us, but that wasn't going to stop us, we had already come so far. Faction 2 lead comfortable lives, it was going to be hard to convince them. We were all tired, hungry and scared of what this revolution may bring, but one thing's for sure, things were going to change…

Let Your True Colours Shine
Rosa Davenport

I wish I was grey. All the other pencils are, but I'm violet. I used to think I was beautiful and that it was amazing to be different. Now I just want to be like all the others: grey. Sure, it's dull and boring, but it's normal so that's what I want to be.

"Go away," they all shout, "you don't belong here!"

Every time they say that, I feel smaller and smaller until I am a tiny stub of a pencil. Sometimes I think that it would be easier to become a rogue, hiding in the classroom and occasionally stealing a sharpener. My biggest hope is to be adopted by a student. They would give me a comfy pencil case and I would finally have a use.

After getting back from our weekly sharpening, the grey pencils decided it was time to take action. And that action was against me. I had known that something was off since yesterday. Most of them had just been as horrible as usual, calling me names and whispering behind my back. But some kept giving me sympathetic looks and nervous smiles.

I should've been happy that they were being nice, but the positive attention just made me uneasy. The leader pulled me aside and whispered, "I'm sorry to have do this, but it's the only way to keep the other pencils' respect."

"What are you doing to me?" I asked urgently, a knot of worry forming in my lead. He glanced nervously around, as if checking that no one was watching, then replied, "We had a meeting last night, and we, ummm.... voted you out".

I felt like I'd been punched in the stomach. I knew they didn't like me, but to go this far – it was just inpencil.

"There's more," he added. "They're going to throw you out of the pot onto the floor!"

I looked down at the sheer drop, and I knew that if I was pushed I would never write again. I heard a cheer coming from the pencil pot, and the leader just had time to warn me to run. I twirled around desperately looking for a place to hide, but it was too late – the mob was upon me! They surged forward and I toppled over the edge. My body split on half in impact and the tip of my lead shattered, leaving me splayed on the floor.

A child picked me up. She gently lifted my broken body and taped me up. She smiled and reached for a drawer. Inside was something I had never imagined in my wildest dreams. It was full of… coloured pencils! They were like me! The girl placed me down next to them and said, "Finally! The full rainbow." I was the missing piece. I, Violet, had completed the rainbow, and found my place.

Inequality
Rebecca Nell

I was only thirteen when I was taken on a journey across seas to get to our new home. Supposedly "lucky" to have been captured together; it couldn't be further from the truth…

It all began the day the white people came, taking us from our village, marching us along the coast. Soon we reached a ship, waiting to escort us "home". I had never seen such a vessel; a jumble of voices speaking an alien language greeted us onboard what would be our residence for the next eight weeks. Curiously, my sister and I were kept above deck. Seeing the haunted images etched on our parents' faces, we understood why.

I won't say much about the journey; the truth is I don't remember much. I recollect having tiny portions of food served at times when the sailors remembered, deep wounds wrapping my parents' wrists. I recall the putrid stench rising from the cabins below and the sleepless nights.

Finally arriving at our destination, I was a changed

person, ill-equipped to deal with the trauma ahead. The auction was quick with slave owners snapping commands at my fellow comrades and dragging them away. As heavy clouds appeared on the horizon, I felt my heart being torn in two; my parents were hauled off in one direction, my sister and I in the other. I promised myself I would get back to them.

But life had to go on. We became established as maids of a rich household, our days filled with endless sweeping, dusting and washing; working from dawn till dusk to keep our masters happy. If we didn't work hard enough, a sharp slap on the wrists would jerk us back to reality. So we worked. What else could we do?

The only distraction was a nearby church. Attending every Sunday, it offered chance of escape. And it was while sitting in the wooden pews, that we first heard the seed – of rebellion. Slaves were angry about their treatment. Fury crouched on the horizon like a tiger; watching and waiting for the right time to unleash its power. You could cut the tension with a knife. This was when we first thought of joining them. Whispers of a protest passed down the aisles. Across town, revolts reverberated. It began in the plantations, men refused to work. Then it spread indoors

— maids ignoring orders. While terrifying, it was equally exciting. Now we had started, we couldn't stop.

As the protests continued, a leader emerged from the rebels, calling a meeting in the town square. As crowds filled the spaces, I spotted a familiar face. The face of my father! Shrieking with delight, we pushed through the crowd towards him, greeting our parents in an embrace. My story got its happy ending — but not everyone's did. This fact inspired me to fight for our rights. However long it had gone on for, slavery was not fair, not right and resulted in an inequality that would plague the world for years to come.

Take a Stand
Zephan Agbim

Racism is wrong,
Wake up and make a change,
Take action quickly,
Be bold and strong,
Stand up and come along,
So where do you begin?
Marches have been taken,
We've all been forsaken.
This is a story,
About winning and glory.

As I walk through the tunnel, I hear loud booing. I feel downhearted and intimidated. I slowly walk onto the pitch, where the atmosphere is overwhelming. I don't know if it is the colour of my skin or the mistakes I've made in the past but I will not let it get to me.

I look around me, my teammates eyeing up the ball. At that moment, as a child I remember walking into my classroom and other children asking me why my skin was so dark. The referee blows his whistle and the match begins.

As a young child, I always dreamed of playing in the World Cup. I would play football anywhere and with anything. I grew up in a poor neighbourhood in Newcastle and I was the only black kid in my class at school. In all my spare time, I played football with my friends in the street. When I didn't get into the school team, I ran home, and I cried in my bed for the rest of the day. I knew it had something to do with the colour of my skin, but I practised every day until I received a letter one day inviting me to a trial for several of the top clubs nearby. I went to the trials and triumphed through to the next round.

I was delighted when Newcastle United offered me a place in their academy. I felt like a star in the sky on a new path to a greater galaxy. At senior level, I had a tough time: crisp packets being thrown at me, people swearing and calling me names, racist abuse and somebody keyed my car. I could not take it, and I said to the fans, "I can't change the way I look." I told myself that I wouldn't go to another tournament, though here I am, at a World Cup final with my head held high and a vest underneath my T-shirt saying, "Show some Respect and Take Action!".

The ball falls to me, midway through the opposition's half, I do a classic move that my hero, Drogba, used to do. I am one-on-one with the keeper, who pulls me to the ground. The referee points to the penalty spot. I step up confidently to take the kick, recalling all the negative past in my career – the pain and the joy. This is my chance to send the world a positive message. I smash the ball with precision, into the bottom corner, and the net bundles. I run to the corner flag and rip my shirt off to show the vest! Life always gives us a chance to take a stand.

The Ballerina
Ella Kitui

"Jada!" Mum shouted. "The letter, it's here!"

Frantically I ran downstairs, my heart pounding like a drum. Trembling with excitement I scanned the envelope. It said National Ballet Company. Mum and I both looked at each other our eyes full of hope. Gruelling try-outs and competitions all lead up to this. Hands shaking my finger slid across the opening on the envelope.

Taking the letter out I read: "Dear Jada Trinity Jones, we are extremely pleased to inform you that you have been accepted into the National Ballet School!"

Screaming echoed through our house and we jumped up and down excitedly. I did it. I really did it. The first lesson started in a week's time which gave us time to buy the uniform. The next day we made our way to the shop and we still couldn't believe that I did it. You could see how proud my mum was, it was radiating off of her.

Entering the shop, we made our way to the tights section to find some flesh-coloured tights. To our disappointment they only had different shades of pink, even though we looked everywhere. Confused, we went to the counter to ask if they had any tights in the shades of black, but he just looked at us confused. At this point my mum was raging inside, a volcano bubbling, how could they not have any tights my skin tone?

Disgusted we left the shop. Mum and I went to every dance shop that we could find but they were all the same. A shadow of doubt entered my head. Was this meant for me? I felt as if I wasn't supposed to be a ballerina that I didn't belong in the dance community. No! I worked hard for my scholarship and I belong.

It finally was the day of my first lesson. After a lot of googling and researching we finally found some tights my colour, but it wasn't easy. As I entered the room, I felt strong, prepared and confident. Quickly we started to warm up and then our teacher put us into a line. Excitement ran through my veins and I was full of adrenaline. As she was looking at everyone, she stopped at me. Yes, I thought she's noticed me. I stood up even taller ready for any criticism but then those 8 words she said to me hit me like a bullet.

"You're going to straighten your hair right? It's so we

can all be the same and you can blend in."

I couldn't believe it. I thought I could have my chance to stand out, be part of something, to feel welcome. All I got was disappointment and people looking at me as if I didn't belong. Just because I wasn't the same as everyone else they thought they could change me to be like them so we were all "uniform".

No! Dance isn't about blending it is about expressing and being yourself.

Racism

Isabel Nyaruwa

There is a monster within,
But is not seen
Sometimes it finds its way out
Mostly hidden in plain sight
The monster loathes diversity
It's oblivious to hurting others
It tramples others success
It will go to the extent of killing someone because they
are DIFFERENT
It mangles your heart and spits it out
Destroying you from within
Spreading its venom to kill its prey
The monster thinks it can treat others differently
Because it believes it is more superior than others
It believes that others aren't as civilised as its breed
Just because the others are DIFFERENT
Even though there is the monster within,
Some have banished the monster and have changed

their ways

They now see that they were wrong

They now see that everyone is EQUAL

The "others" are fighting for equality

Fighting for their freedom

The monster has been alive for centuries

It is time to stop the monster

I am one of the others

I am DIFFERENT

I am Anguished

I am Devastated

I am pained for all I have seen

But... I have HOPE

I believe that the monster's beliefs are wrong

No one should be treated differently because of who they are

Everyone is equal and should be treated the same

Black lives matter.

Drumbeat
Laurie Wardill-Bartlett

For a long time, life in my village was good. But then came the darkness. Then came the storm. Or, as you might put it, the British arrived. Under the cover of dusk, they stole into our settlement and captured a group of tribes people. Then, for good measure, they burnt the village to the ground. Amongst the loot that they took back to their ship was me, and when they reached it, I was presented as a gift to the captain, a large man with a nasty smile and a nastier laugh.

The ship itself was an old wreck; the planks from which it was made were rotting, the sails smelled musty and the entire structure was a seething mass of rats. But worst of all were the cargo holds. That was where they kept the slaves. There were around six hundred slaves on that boat, and each of them was chained to a plank-bed with one toilet bucket to share between about forty of them. The stench was awful.

Worse still, on days when the sea was particularly rough, the captain would order the sailors to shut the portholes, leaving the slaves gasping for air. Many of them got seasick at times like those, but I would prefer not to go into details. The days went by slowly, and throughout most of them I was kept in the captain's quarters. Only, every afternoon, I was taken out onto the deck and beaten by a sailor.

All the slaves were forced to dance to the slow, dull beat, and anyone who stepped even slightly out of rhythm was lashed with the cat o'nines. Of course, we were all thinking about the days when we were free to make our own music — the colourful mix of short beats and lyrical pipes that we had enjoyed so often.

During the later part of our long and dreadful voyage, two of the slaves, both from my village, were allowed on deck for a while. Their hands were bound together, but even still, as soon as they had the chance, they jumped overboard. I guess even death was a better option than staying on that boat. I just wish the others were as lucky. When we arrived in America, the slaves were sold to a tobacco plantation's owner and put to work in the fields. The last time I saw them, they were being led away, taken to a life of sorrow and despair.

Then the captain sold me to an old man who put me in a cart and drove me back to his home. But, as soon as he got there, he put me in a darkened attic filled with crates and cobwebs. The man must have forgotten about me, as I stayed there for a long time. I don't know how long. But, in 1753, I was found and taken to the British museum. That's where I am now.

Oh, and, in case you're wondering, I'm a drum.

Welcome Home
Evelyn Williams

"Welcome home Social Experiment 0211! Utopolis has been designed for you to live in for the rest of your lives, you will never want to leave!" blasted through the radio as our convoy drove towards the gates, where I could see millions of trucks waiting for permission to enter.

The Overseer had promised us a utopian adventure. As the one-hundred metre gates opened, I excitedly peered out my window expecting to see luxurious lemonade fountains, grand buildings beyond my imagination and an ice-cream store on every corner! The groggy, dusty fog cleared as the eerie, rusty gates fully opened revealing this was nothing like our home back in LA, or the utopia promised.

This place was different, the surrounding land was dead, no trees, no grass and no animals. At the side of the road stood millions of people of colour, like me, waiting to be processed. It was becoming clear that this was an elaborate plan gathering us out of the way, to stop us revolting. Other than the pounding noises coming from the convoy vans tyres and the blaring tannoys there was nothing else to be heard. The sky was grey with thick black clouds trudging by. There were guards patrolling the walls, controlling what went in and what came out.

Eventually we arrived at our new home and it was then that I knew life would never be the same again. And I was right… I have noticed some very odd goings on. There are army vans at the end of every street during the night but by sunrise they are gone with no trace of them ever being there. Sometimes I would hear stories of how people would try to escape, however, I'm not sure if they did.

Occasionally, if you listen hard enough you hear their screams fading into the night. Their screams haunt me to this day. Last night I followed a van on a makeshift bike I created out of spare parts, all the way to an abandoned facility on the edge of town. I never would've followed it if it didn't contain my best friend Filippe.

The van entered through a large back door into a garage. I paused to think about what I would do next. I decided that it would be best for me to turn around and come back in the daylight. Just as I was about to turn, someone grabbed me from behind tightly on my shoulders. They beat me to the ground and I slowly slipped into unconsciousness.

When I awoke, I was strapped to a cold, metal table, paralysed. I then noticed Filippe was attached to the table opposite me with dried blood staining his forehead. My name is Samir Salah, I am an Egyptian-American teenager growing up in one of the toughest times for people of colour. And I fear I do not have much time left.

2020 Hindsight
Maurice Griffin

It was getting late, but as usual Skye was doing her best to pretend she wasn't really about to fall asleep.

"Pllleeeaaaase, Daddy? Just one last one?" she said, sitting up.

"OK, which one? It can even be a long one," he said, smiling.

"This one! This one! This one!" she said happily, dropping a book in her father's lap and launching herself into bed.

"This one?" he said. Skye's father looked down at the book and ran his fingers over the title. "I'd forgotten about this one. 2020: The Year the World Changed."

"What is it about, Daddy?" Skye said, looking at him oddly.

"Well it's about a time long before you were born," he chuckled. "It is when people judged others because of their skin colour."

Skye shrugged her shoulders and held out her hands

in question.

"The year the world changed," he started. "Covid-19 was first on our list, grasping our country with a full fist. From China it travelled contagion unfurled, we couldn't have known it would damage our world. We went into lockdown, using less stuff. Less plastic less petrol, was this enough? To rescue our planet, was this the first stage, To save our environment, start a new page? In 2020 the last major change, something that in 2050 seems so strange.

"They saw dark skin as a negative, policemen were brutal, their actions insensitive. A man called George Floyd, a father of four, was stopped by police just outside a store. His neck was forced down by a leg. 'I can't breathe!' he would beg. For over eight minutes that knee pushed down some, he coughed and spluttered and begged for his mum.

"At the disgusting death of George Floyd, the officer thought he could avoid being blamed for the end of a black man's life, and the heartbreak of four kids and a wife. But Floyd's life and death started a huge row. People would take a knee and people would bow. Racism had taken a huge bend. Was this finally to be the end? Now gone is the hatred and racist chatter, and we live in a world where Black Lives Matter."

Her dad closed the book softly. Skye smiled and turned over to face the window.

"Did people do really do that?" Skye said yawning, her eyes slowly closing.

Skye's father closed the book and bent over to kiss her head. "Well, not everyone, but some people were blind to prejudice and didn't even realise how hurtful their behaviour was."

He leaned on the door frame and turned out the light. "It's odd that 2020 was the year the rules distanced us, but in the end, it was the year that brought us together. Good night, Skye."

THE END

We Shall Rise
Iris Trewhitt

"Okay. I can do this." Kara was fidgeting in her chair, her eyes closed thinking. She was applying for the job of Captain Of Deporian Warriors. This was her only chance.

"Kara Miller!" commanded the voice from the speakers.

Kara sighed and walked over to the large, wooden doors that were soon to let her into the room where her dream could come true.

"Hello, my name is Kara Miller, I am African-American and I live in square six. I really want this job. I think I would be a great captain because…"

"Next!"

"B-but!" Kara stuttered.

"I said NEXT!"

Kara stumbled out. "Don't cry! Don't let them see that they've got to you!"

She took a deep breath and pushed the doors to the interview room open. "Permission to speak to the Panelte."

"Granted!"

"You have no idea what my experience is! It's completely unfair!" argued Kara.

"Leave! How dare you speak to us like that!" they replied, and one of them slapped her across the face.

Stunned she ran. Tep! Tep! echoed her feet every time her boots hit the floor. She tripped. Darkness consumed her.

"Wake up! You're blocking the way!" Tiffany the blonde-haired, blue-eyed successful candidate was pulling her up, her sparkling captain badge glared in the sunlight, blinding her.

"So, did you get it?" questioned a friendly voice.

Kara ignored it and flopped onto her bed.

"I will take that as a no," came the voice again. It was Mala, Kara's best friend.

That night Kara couldn't sleep. She felt empty. She felt lonely. She felt unaccepted. She got out of bed and picked up her backpack. If this is how they are going to treat me just because of my colour, then they are down one warrior.

SHHK! Went the old, grubby window as Kara opened it.

"What are you doing, Kara? It's three in the morning!" whispered Mala.

"Errrm... I am just a bit hot, go back to sleep!" replied Kara.

Mala nodded sleepily and flopped back into her pillow, asleep in seconds.

Kara clambered out of the window and took a last look at her lifelong friend. How sad life was going to be without her. Sneaking through the security she kept on thinking: "Mala. I miss you already."

Once she reached the edge of the forest, she pulled up her hood and didn't look back. Whilst Kara was gathering sticks to make a fire she could only think about how unequal The Paneltes had been to her.

"Maybe The Paneltes need enlightening?" was the thought that hit her hard, as the fire flickered. As she bit into her bread she knew that she needed to make sure she saw Mala again. The next morning Kara woke up knowing she had to go back. She knew there needed to be change. She knew that everyone else who is black needed to be treated the same.

"We shall rise!" And she marched back to the city.

Equality Matters
Kelsey Hamilton

I forced myself to run, faster and faster until my exhausted feet barely skimmed the pavement: I darted down an alleyway, completely concealed from the street, and collapsed onto the dusty ground. My heart pulsated rapidly in my chest as I felt my body tremble in fear. Why wasn't I more cautious?

The narrow passageway was dead, it seemed as if nobody had stepped foot down it for centuries, and the abhorrent metallic smell only worsened my nausea. The roaring hollers of the people sent violent shivers down my spine – the broad-shouldered blue men swept through the street, their huge black boots ricocheting on the roads. They were gone.

Silence invaded the once rowdy street: it enclosed me like a thick blanket, roaring in my ears, and I desperately clamped my hands on either side of my whirling head. Embracing my knees against my chest, I could feel my heart thudding, like a rhythmic drum, seemingly bringing me a sense of comfort and warmth in the darkening alley. A tidal wave of emotions overwhelmed me as I rested my throbbing head onto my knees, so that I was curled into a tight bubble of protection. Tears prickled my eyes; they refused to stay hidden, and waterfalls of sorrow cascaded down my cheeks. They tasted bitter, like droplets of pure poison burning my dark skin, an unwanted reminder of the pain I was experiencing.

Why was I, just an innocent girl, being mistreated just because of my race? Why was I discriminated against, and seen as a threat? Why was I frightened to walk down my street, in case I was treated brutally by policemen? Why was my race and my skin targeted and treated differently? What did I do to deserve this treatment? A hurricane of questions penetrated my mind, yet for none of them I could think of an answer.

Uncurling from my position, I attempted to calm my breathing, yet my tears were stubborn, now huge uncontrollable drops sliding off my cheeks. I outstretched one of my arms, gently inspecting it, although it was a different colour to white skin, I saw no difference. Then I repeated the process with my other arm, my skin was a different colour, yet I still saw no different. They were still normal arms. My skin was black, yet it was still skin. We all bleed the same crimson blood, and we all breathe the same oxygen. So why is my race treated differently?

Suddenly, a growing noise filled the street – I snapped out of my daydream to the yells and cries of crowds. Apprehensive, I shrank into the darkness like a terrified mouse, as a shadow loomed over the alley. Squeezing my eyes shut, I was surprised when a pale hand was offered out to me, helping my paralysed body stand. A girl my age smiled at me compassionately: in one hand she clutched a large banner, reading "Black Lives Matter".

"A princess like you should not be discriminated against."

At the Age of
Saumyah Singh

My name is… actually that's not important, but my story
is. When I was 5, we left Sierra Leone and travelled a long
journey all the way to England, for my mum's job. I joined a
new school and in Year 1 made a few friends. There were
some strange, big changes to my life at the time but I got
used to it pretty quickly!

At the age of 7, my favourite thing to do was to play
with barbie dolls! I wanted to look like one, that's how
much I adored them. My friends and I would bring our
Barbies into school and talk about which doll looked similar
to which girl. All of my friends had a doll that looked like
them but not me… Why didn't any of those barbie dolls
look like me? Why were they all light skinned?

I soon grew out of my barbie phase and completely
forgot about them. At the age of ten, I had a passion to do
realistic drawings of people, and I loved to colour them in
too. One day I tried to draw myself, and I asked my friend
for a skin coloured pencil. She didn't reply so I look up at

her, and she looked back at me in confusion. There was a skin coloured pencil for white people but not for black people? I never finished that drawing.

At the age of eleven, I joined high school! There were a few more black people than at primary school but not too many. When I joined, I quickly realised that people aren't always kind. Nobody ever said anything racist directly to my face, but the racism was always there. Whether it was "just a joke" or "word". I'm lucky nobody ever physically hurt me though.

At the age of fifteen, I started wearing make-up, but I soon realised that there wasn't a shade of foundation for my skin colour. The range for lighter skin colour was large, but when I looked for foundation for my tone the "range" only consisted of three different colours. Not even the biggest companies had a skin tone for everyone.

At the age of twenty-one I was shopping in a store. The employees were following me around the shop and watching me weirdly. After a while I became uncomfortable, so I turned around and asked the employee why he was following me. He replied "just for safety!" I left the shop and didn't come back.

In the year of 2020, an unarmed black man named

George Floyd was brutally killed by being restrained by the police. His death sparked many people to fight for Black Lives Matter. On social media, the news, and protests. The movement has not just spread in the USA, it is spreading worldwide. People are listening, things are changing. Solutions are being made, problems are being solved. We all have a voice, and we need to use it for the good, make your own story...

Innocence
Nkosazana Khawula

"Officer, please!" I scream, my voice hoarse from the lack of oxygen. The man in blue ignores me, pushing my head into the pavement even harder than he was just mere seconds ago. Arms behind my back, hands trapped in handcuffs, stripping my freedom away from me. Then, I hear her voice.

"Michael!? That's my son! Let go of him, please!" My mother's desperate, heart-wrenching cries are caught on various smartphones as the police hold her back. An officer pulls out a gun, aiming at my mother. Panic takes over my body as I realise that my mother's in danger. I struggle and try to resist, to protect the woman that has loved me ever since I was born. But I can't, I can't. I can't.

"Don't do it! Don't kill her, kill me!" I plead and my sobs are caught in my throat. I feel pain everywhere, my lungs, my legs, my arms and the most excruciating pain is in my heart. The man pinning me to the ground was supposed to help me. I was scared for my life when a white man pulled out a gun and aimed it at me, and this is the result of breaking that one rule that every single black person must know. Never call the police if you're in trouble. Call a relative, friend, anyone. Anyone but the police or else they'll kill you.

A loud bang rings in my ears as I assume that I've just been shot, but I don't feel any pain. I open my eyes hesitantly, praying to see my mother safe and healthy. She jumps back, an officer shot a bullet just inches away from her foot, a warning shot. This is all my fault. I should've never called the police.

Suddenly, a white man steps out from the crowd, anger written on his face. The officers are silent as he steps closer, stopping as he begins to shout.

"Officers, how dare you pin an innocent man to the ground!? Take your hands off of this man and release him! He did nothing wrong. He called you because he was afraid. He was scared of that man that was going to hurt him!" The officers freeze, and surprisingly, they let me go. I hug the man that just saved my life and thank him.

"And he lived happily ever after! That was the story of your grandfather, kids. Now get to bed!" my grandma exclaims, smiling at us as she hugs us both tightly.

My brother does as she says, but I stay put. "That

white man didn't really help. They killed grandad, didn't they?" I question.

My grandma freezes, tears leaving her eyes as she frowns. She shakes her head slowly, grief in her eyes.

"Yes, you're right dear," she whispers back as she steps towards me, wrapping her loving arms around me. "Go to sleep now, okay?"

I nod, turning to run upstairs, joining my brother in the bathroom to prepare for bed.

Hands Where I Can See Them
Ella Rose Palmer

"Stop."

The words cut into me like knives, piercing my skin. I turned around with my hands above my head. Overwhelmed by the police, flashing lights and guns, I dropped to my knees. I took rapid breaths and my eyes squinted as a bright light was shined harshly in them.

"Get up."

The owner of the voice wore a blue uniform, complete with a badge and sneer. I knew what to do. I stood up, lifted my arms above my head and stared at the ground. My heart beat so fast that I thought it would shatter but I knew what to do. Do what they say. Don't run, don't move quickly, don't answer back. Moving makes the police nervous, Dad told me. Put your hands where they can see them, he said. Put your hands exactly where they can see them.

"Stop."

I'd heard of police stopping cars but I never thought

it would happen to me. Yawning, I got out my car and pulled out my ID. I squinted as an officer shone a light in our eyes – I was too tired for this. Suddenly, I noticed Rue trembling. She stood with her hands in the air as an officer pointed his gun and his torch in her face. I quickly recoiled as I saw the smirk that he wore, accompanied by the reflection of the blue and red flashing lights burning in his eyes. He seemed to delight in holding us by gunpoint for no reason at all, maybe it made him feel powerful, invincible.

But then I realised something. He didn't seem to enjoy holding "us" by gun point – no, he hadn't said a word to me since we got pulled over. Instead, he seemed to delight in terrifying Rue. Deep breaths, I told myself. Slowly, I raised my eye line and defiantly looked the officer in the eyes.

"We didn't do anything wrong," I began to say, never breaking eye contact, never giving him a reason to get angry.

"Shut up!" he yelled, pushing me against the car door. "Put your hands behind your head!" He shouted again. I saw the cold hard stare he gave me; one of hatred and contempt. I saw how I looked in his eyes, disgusting. To him, I was nothing.

I watched in horror as the officer pushed Rue against

the car door. But I couldn't just stand by, I needed to do something!

"Let her go!" I shouted loudly. "She didn't do anything wrong!"

The officer looked in my direction and suddenly I didn't feel so big. I saw his gun. He slowly began to saunter in my direction.

"You," he spat at me, "can go home."

I was confused – what had either of us done?

"She's... different," he said with a smirk. But the only difference I could see between us was our skin colour. Indignation filled my eyes, but before I knew what was happening, he'd dragged Rue into his car and they were gone.

317

EXTRA
BITS

OXFORD CORPUS CHILDREN'S LANGUAGE REPORT 2020

Since 2012 a group of very clever people at Oxford University Press has looked at the language used by children for the '500 Words' competition as part of their ongoing research into language written for and by children. This year, they've looked closely at the stories submitted by children to '500 Words: Black Lives Matter 2020', and here are some of the most interesting findings from their research:

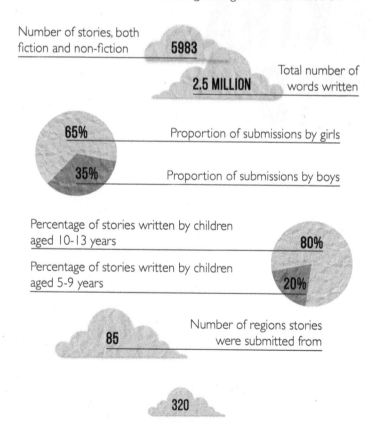

Number of stories, both fiction and non-fiction — **5983**

2.5 MILLION — Total number of words written

65% — Proportion of submissions by girls

35% — Proportion of submissions by boys

Percentage of stories written by children aged 10-13 years — **80%**

Percentage of stories written by children aged 5-9 years — **20%**

85 — Number of regions stories were submitted from

Some other really fascinating facts:

- For '500 Words: BLM' the most used name was George Floyd. Before, the top famous names for 8 years running were Santa and Cinderella.
- BLM is a new word not previously recorded in children's writing.
- Other words that were used a lot included protest, racism, racist, equal and rights.
- The word protest was used a whopping 3730% more than in '500 Words 2020'.
- There were more 'happy' words than 'sad' words used in '500 Words: BLM' with 62% of words being classed as 'happy' and only 38% classed as 'sad'. This is slightly lower than '500 Words 2020' with 68% 'happy' words and 32% 'sad' words.
- Loads of positive messages can be seen in the stories, with fantastic phrases like 'proud to be black' and 'proud to be me' used more times than previously.
- In other children's writing the word colour appears in the context of describing things like the sun / gleaming white teeth / a peach / carrots / snow / rainbow / the sky / deep, blue sea. In '500 Words: BLM', colour is mainly used in the context of the colour of my/your/ their skin.

The findings of this report reflect the inventiveness of children today as well as their empathy and engagement with serious issues and campaigns.

500 Words: Black Lives Matter data and insights are from the Oxford Children's Corpus* and the Children's Dictionaries and Children's Language department at Oxford University Press.

*The Oxford Children's Corpus is a growing database of writing for and by children developed and maintained by Oxford University Press for the purpose of children's language research.

MALORIE BLACKMAN: WRITING TIPS

Writing stories is about the exploration of your main character's life through their actions, thoughts and feelings. Writing is such a wonderful way to create. You can create new people, new situations, even new worlds if you want to. What do you want to write about? Is there a particular topic or subject matter that appeals to you? Is there an idea you want to investigate? Then go for it!

You can create characters to put into a situation to see how they would cope, what they would do. Maybe create characters who are the complete opposite to you in a number of ways to explore their actions and reactions to the many obstacles they have to overcome in your story. I always say that creating new characters is a great way to live many lives at once as it feels like everything that happens to my characters happens to me as well – the good, the bad and the ugly. I feel the joy and the sadness that my characters experience. That can sometimes make writing uncomfortable but always rewarding.

Do you have a favourite space or place? Maybe you could create a character or characters to explore that place which could be a moment in time. Remember, your main character doesn't have to be human. It could be an animal, an alien from another planet, a legendary creature, a person with special powers, even a made-up creature. Or maybe the place itself could be a character.

How does your character speak? Do they have a particular way of expressing themselves? Have fun with exploring the different ways your characters could do that. They don't need to structure their sentences in the same way that you do.

What does your character do? Who are they at the start of your story and how are they different at the end? What happens to them to make them different? What do they want at the start of the story? What is stopping them from getting it? How do they overcome all the obstacles in their way? Do they do it on their own? Do they have help? Are they resentful or grateful for any help they receive? What have they learned – if anything – by the end of the story? Have they helped others along the way, or have they only helped themselves? Have their opinions and/or attitudes changed by the time the story finishes? These are all questions to keep in mind when creating your story. You don't need to answer all of them. Maybe it's enough to answer just one of them. It's your story so it's entirely up to you.

Most importantly, have fun. If you enjoy writing your story, we're more likely to enjoy reading it. If your characters surprise you, make you laugh, make you cry, make you gasp, make you think, then hopefully that's what they'll do to us too. Enjoy yourself.

Happy writing!

Malorie Blackman

FRANK COTTRELL-BOYCE: WRITING TIPS

First: switch on your computer.

NO! Don't touch that power button! Trying to write on a computer is like trying to paint your nails on a log flume. Too many distractions! You need a pen and a piece of paper and somewhere comfy to sit.

Second: make sure that before you start you have a brilliant idea...

NOOO!! Don't wait. People always ask writers where they get their ideas from and they always lie about it. The secret truth is... great ideas for stories come WHILE YOUR WRITING. So grab any old idea. Steal one. It doesn't matter. I absolutely promise you that five minutes after you've started, you'll start having better ideas.

Third: plan everything very carefully. Maybe draw a graph or a mind map.

NOOOO!!! Don't do that. You're writing a story not building an airport. Just dive in and have fun. If it goes wrong you can always start again. You don't need a plan. You just need to sit down and do it.

Fourth: always check the spelling before you write a word down and make sure your handwriting is neat.

NOOOOO!!!! Seriously we don't care about the spelling. And don't worry about making it neat. You're going to rewrite this anyway so you can be as scruffy as you like.

Fifth: when you're finished take care to hide your story away so that no one can steal your idea.

NOOOOOOO!!!!!! That's a seven "o" seven exclamation mark no. The loudest no of all. Because the very best thing you can do with your story is to share it. And you begin sharing it by reading it out loud. Read it to someone you trust. If you don't trust anyone but yourself read it out loud to yourself. Maybe record yourself reading it and then play it back. But whatever you do make sure you read it out loud. Reading a story out loud is the very best way in the world ever of finding out whether it works or not. Read it out loud.

Sixth: when you're reading it out loud you'll find that some bits work and some bit don't. Keep the bits that work and fix the bits that don't.

Yes. That's completely right.

Now go and write.

Frank Cottrell-Boyce

FRANCESCA SIMON: WRITING TIPS

I hope these fantastic stories inspire you to write your own. Here are some tips to get you started.

Finish what you start. Don't just write lots of beginnings. Try writing the end first, THEN the beginning and the middle if you're stuck.

Writing in the first person is easier than writing in the third. But remember, WHO your narrator is influences HOW they tell the story. The robber will tell the story very differently from the policewoman who catches him.

Ideas are everywhere. Keep a notebook and jot down anything that strikes you. A thought. A dream. A joke. A bit of dialogue.

Think of the story as a journey. How is your character different at the end from the beginning? What's happened to them to make this change? The middle of a story is what I call the TWIST – what causes your character's life to change? Ask lots of questions. The answers will be your story.

Another way to create a character is to ask yourself questions to find out who they are. Where do they live? What do they look like? Who are their friends? Who are their enemies? What do they care about? And, most important, what do they WANT more than anything? And WHO or WHAT is stopping them getting what they want? For example, Cinderella wants more than anything…to go to the ball. What's stopping her is poverty and her mean, horrible step-sisters.

The main way I develop my characters is through dialogue. Let HOW your characters speak reveal what they're like. For example, Horrid Henry and Perfect Peter. I put them into lots of different situations, and I listen to what they say and write it down.

Here they are, fighting as usual.

'Don't call me Ugly, Toad!'

'Don't call me Toad, Ugly!'

This tells you we are listening to two brothers who fight all the time. Who call each other names. Who are aggressive.

Or listen to this:

'You're the meanest parents in the world and I hate you!' shrieked Horrid Henry.

'You're the best parents in the world and I love you,' said Perfect Peter.

This tells you how competitive they are and how much sibling rivalry they have.

I think of characters as people I want to get to know, and who want to get to know me. So say hi to them, and hear what they have to say.

Another great way to come up with a good idea is to mix up different types of story. For example:

Ghost	Mystery	History	Horror
Family	Detective	Science-	Romance
Comedy	School	fiction	Magic
Animal	Fantasy	Sports	Fairy tale

Now mix up two (or more) of them. Horror/romance could be two zombies who fall in love. Science fiction/detective could be a time traveller from the future who solves modern mysteries. School/Magic could be a school for witches or wizards or geniis or vampires or unicorns...

Happy reading (and writing!)

Francesca Simon

CHARLIE HIGSON: WRITING TIPS

ONCE UPON A TIME

People are always arguing about what makes human beings different to other animals. Are we cleverer? Well, recent research shows that birds are pretty smart, actually – even chickens are cleverer than anyone thought (although I've never seen one on University Challenge.) Are we the only creatures to use language, then? Maybe... but bees have a way of communicating by doing a little dance, chimps use sign language, and birds use Twitter.

I think the thing that makes us different is that we're the only ones to tell stories. Humans make sense of the world by telling stories about it. It's how we understand people and history and our emotions... everything. And each of our lives is a story in itself.

I've been lucky enough to make a living telling stories. Yes – I'm basically paid to make stuff up. But we all do it all the time. We tell stories about our day, about what someone said to us, about a funny thing that happened at the weekend. And think of the stories you can't forget, how they will always be with you.

I hope you enjoy the stories in this book, and I hope they inspire you to write some stories of your own. Because it's fun and it's what makes us human. Actually, I've just had an idea for a good start to a story. 'There was this chicken, and she always dreamed of going on University Challenge...'

ABOUT CORAM BEANSTALK

Our mission is to create a generation of readers for life who have the skills and confidence to reach their true potential, whatever their life circumstances. Too often too many children are left behind. We want to change this.

That's why we recruit, train and support volunteers to give one-to-one reading support to help children aged 3-13 to become confident, passionate and able readers. These are often children who, for whatever reason, may have become disengaged with reading and can find it a struggle.

As a result of our forty-seven years of experience in creating readers, we are also able to offer a series of training programmes both to the wider community and directly to educational settings, for people who want to help their own children, or other children they read with, to learn to read for pleasure whilst improving reading skills.

In partnership with The Black Lives Matter 500 Words we want to ensure those children from the BAME communities are supported even more. With any funds raised we will seek out more partner schools to ensure we reach the most disadvantaged BAME children. We will also recruit more volunteers from these communities to help us in our work.

We also know how important it is to engage children in reading that they see themselves reflected in the books they are offered. We are committed to providing a diverse range of inclusive titles and any funds raised will help us to increase the books we offer.

Together we can help children on a path to becoming a reader.

WITH THANKS

PUBLISHERS:
    Atlantic
    Bonnier Books UK
    Canongate
    Faber & Faber
    Hachette UK
    HarperCollins UK
    Pan Macmillan
    Oxford University Press
    Profile
    Puffin (an imprint of Penguin Random House)
    Studio Press (an imprint of Bonnier Books UK)
    Simon & Schuster

RETAIL:
    Amazon Alexa   WHSmith

MEDIA:
    News UK   Virgin Radio UK

HOSTS / JUDGES:
    Angellica Bell   Michael Underwood

JUDGES:
    Malorie Blackman OBE   Francesca Simon
    Charlie Higson   Frank Cottrell-Boyce

500 WORDS: BLACK LIVES MATTER

READERS:

Nicole Kidman
Mark Strong
David Tennant
Shobna Gulati
Gugu Mbatha-Raw

Jim Broadbent
Amanda Abbington
Rob Brydon
Stephen Graham
Sanjeev Bhaskar

SUPPORTERS:

Charlie Mackesy
Aasmah Mir
Adam Kay
Adam Woodyat
Adil Ray
Amanda Abbington
Barney Harwood
Beverley Knight
Candice Brown
Christian Williams
Colin Jackson
Dawn French
David Suchet
Denise Welch
Dr Ranj
Emma Barton
Fay Ripley
Gaby Roslin
Giovanna and Tom
   Fletcher
Helen George
Hermione Norris
Holly Willoughby

Jake Wood
Joe Wicks
Kellie Shirley
Konnie Huq
John Pienaar
Jamie Murray
Judy Murray
Nicki Chapman
Noel Clarke
Noma Dumezweni
Ortis Deley
Paterson Joseph
Paula Radcliffe
Rachel Horne
Sam Pinkham
Sanjeev Bhaskar
Shobna Gulati
Simon Thomas
Stephen Graham
Tanya Franks
F2Freestylers, Billy
   Wingrove and Jeremy
   Lynch

MEDIA:

The Sun / Sun Online
The i Paper / iNews
Metro.co.uk
Mirror Online
Daily Star Online
Express Online
BBC News Online
Press Association
The Sunday Times
Sky News
Times Radio
BBC Radio London
The British Blacklist
The Voice Online

Heat Magazine
Hello! Magazine
Sky FYI
CBBC Newsround
First News
LADbible
The Lady Online
Good Housekeeping
  Online
Scala Radio Online
Tech Advisor
The Bookseller
My Baba
Raring 2 Go

VIRGIN RADIO AND NEWS UK & VIRGIN RADIO BREAKFAST:

Scott Taunton
Nick Daly
Mike Cass
Meera Depala
Jayne Cheeseman
Vassos Alexander
Rachel Horne
John Dutton
Claire Telford
Anthony Shaw
Gareth Iles

Richard Andrews
Brett Water
Tom Ross
Helen Everett
Kejal Kamani
David Brain
Georgie Redmayne
Daisy Dunlop
Chris Taylor
Rebecca Brooks

AMAZON/AUDIBLE:

Phil Ray Smith
Tom Killian
Katie Fitzpatrick

& their colleagues at
Amazon and Audible

500 WORDS: BLACK LIVES MATTER

FREUD COMMUNICATIONS:

Matthew Freud
Sean Pritchard
Arlo Brady
David Cummins

Sal Porter
Kate Lee
Vicky Grayson

500 WORDS:

Hiten Vora
Ruby Newman
Nick Aston
Kyle Rowe
Amelia Madan
Suzi Purdie
Vicki Perrin

Helen Thomas
Bob Shennan
Robert Elms
Helen Freeman
Tim Stansbie
Matthew Glubb & all at
  MadeByKite

BONNIER BOOKS UK:

Amy Llambias
Anastasia Ulyanova
Elise Burns
Frankie Jones
Helen Wicks
Jon Perdoni
Kate Manning

Kieran Hood
Laura Pollard
Lizz Skelly
Paul Baxter
Perminder Mann
Sophia Akhtar
Rob Ward

And a big thank you to the hundreds of public judges and to all the children who submitted stories.